MYSTICISM—
The Journey Within

ROBERT CHANEY

ASTARA'S LIBRARY OF MYSTICAL CLASSICS
Astara, Upland, California   91786

A MESSAGE FROM ASTARA

Since 1951 Astara has been reaching to "the whole person" with printed teachings, audio and visual meditation aids, seminars, workshops and retreats. With each passing year, the *Library of Mystical Classics* (of which this book is one volume) has gained growing favor among students of Mystical Christianity, the Ancient Wisdom Teachings, psychic research, metaphysics and related fields.

A booklet titled *Finding Your Place in the Golden Age* is available without cost to persons interested in Astara's publications. You may obtain a copy simply for the asking. Address your request to: Astara Information Office, 800 West Arrow Highway, Upland, Ca. 91786.

LIBRARY OF MYSTICAL CLASSICS

As one of its services to members and nonmembers alike, Astara publishes a series of books under the general title **Astara's Library of Mystical Classics**. A partial list follows. For added information, inquire at your bookstore or address your inquiry to Astara's New Leaf Book Store at 800 West Arrow Highway, Upland, CA 91786.

Beyond Tomorrow — Includes prophecies about war, economics, UFOs, pole shifts, visitors from space; how to create a personal "armor of light," by Earlyne Chaney.

Initiation in the Great Pyramid — Unlock the door to another time through an actual experience in the Great Pyramid. Work with all three selves, extract the vital force of manna, harmonize levels of consciousness, by Earlyne Chaney.

Inner Way, The — Special meditations for healing, self-confidence, stability, creativity, everyday problems of all kinds, by Robert Chaney.

Kundalini and the Third Eye — Mystical, esoteric, psychic and historical; ancient rituals; yogic and breathing techniques; 70 illustrations, by Earlyne Chaney and William Messick.

Make It An Adventure — Helps you shape your mind and abilities, grow in spirit and rid yourself of daily irritations, by Marcus Bach

Masters and Astara, The — Relates the Ancient Wisdom to modern mysticism and the search for God and Self, gives steps to initiation, and a knowledge of the Mystery Schools, by Earlyne Chaney.

Psalms, Prayer Power for Your Problems — Century old ways to use the Psalms to help solve problems, change conditions and heal illnesses. Contains the Psalms in metre, plus additional metaphysical and mystical insights, by Carrie Pevarnik and Robert Chaney.

Remembering, The Autobiography of a Mystic — A startling story of life after death, reincarnation, psychic phenomena; the autobiography of one of Astara's founders, by Earlyne Chaney.

Revelations of Things to Come — The future through 2000 and further; ancient and modern space gods; Doomsday or Coming Light? 40 illustrations, by Earlyne Chaney.

Secrets from Mt. Shasta — A suspenseful spiritual journey to the higher spheres to participate in an initiation, complete with illustrations and photos, by Earlyne Chaney.

Unfolding the Third Eye — An adventure into the superconscious realm of the Self with special techniques for psychic as well as spiritual development, by Robert Chaney.

CONTENTS

ACKNOWLEDGMENTS

The author and the publishers wish to express appreciation for editorial assistance to Sita and Earlyne Chaney, and to Loulie Sprague for the cover photo.

PREFACE

This book is the outgrowth of a series of classes in Christian Mysticism which I taught to graduate students at the College of Oriental Studies in Los Angeles. It discusses a subject which cannot be written about. Why then attempt to do so? There are two reasons.

One is that each person who has a mystical experience of any kind is moved by an inner compulsion to tell others about it. When the blind men were healed they were charged, "See that no man know it." But the experience— so exhilarating, so much like wine fermenting in a bottle until the inner pressure bursts the cork—could not be kept secret. The market crowd was soon treated to the startling spectacle of two formerly blind men shouting to all the world, "I'm healed! I can see!"

The second reason is that many have requested a book which offers organized guidelines toward mystical experiences, guidelines which:

list specific mystical occurences

describe methods to attain them

direct the individual toward the methodology
    best suited to his or her personality

give significant general information to provide
    a solid foundation for the Great Search.

The mysticism I write about in this book could be presented from the viewpoint of any religion ever known. The principles are so universal that they know no boundaries of man-made systems.

I do consider myself a universal religionist in the sense that I accept all religions in their mystical context. For the purpose of this book I present mysticism from the Christian viewpoint. The scriptures of Judaism, Islam, Hinduism, Buddhism, Taoism or others could have served equally well.

There are two ways to approach mysticism: *doctrinal,* a purely intellectual point of view; or *experiential,* the standpoint of personal experience.

We'll explore both in this book.

Because my personal preference is for the experiential, I naturally emphasize it. Therefore, each chapter contains suggestions and techniques to help you personally experience the mystical occurrences discussed in that chapter.

Seekers are too often disappointed because nothing experiential or phenomenal results from their interest in mysticism. "I've meditated," one will say, "but nothing happened and there've been no changes in my life." Such one looks at the handfull of seeds gathered along the way but fails to see the flowers inherent in them. On the mystical planes as well as on the physical, the soil must be prepared, the seed planted and nurtured.

So in this book I propose to offer practical techniques for nurturing your mystical garden—with your consciousness as the soil and mystical ideas as the seed. Perhaps, given thoughtful and proper care, it may become your personal Garden of Eden.

* * * * *

CHAPTER 1

GOD—ARE YOU REALLY THERE?

"Moreover, something is or seems
    That touches me with mystic gleams,
Like glimpses of forgotten dreams.

"Of something felt, like something here;
    Of something done, I know not where;
Such as no language may declare."

—Tennyson.

Does Reality with a capital "R" really exist? And if It does, can finite me have the privilege of an interior association with that Reality?

Am I finite only—or am I in truth a finite-Infinite being—a limited point in space where the unlimited God is focalized into a Presence I can literally sense and know? And perhaps even be helped by?

Many years ago—shortly after graduating from high school, as I recall it—a friend and I were riding in a car and discussing the philosophy of life with what we considered much wisdom. Suddenly, what seemed to be a wild extraneous thought struck me. "Wouldn't it be strange," I wondered aloud, "if we were atoms in the body of God?"

The question seemed to foster the feeling. There descended upon me a sudden sense of profound certainty that I really was some kind of living cell existing as part of a

9

Universal organism, also living, omniscient, omnipotent, and omnipresent.

My consciousness of riding in the car, the presence of my friend, the passing countryside, all seemed dreamlike, almost unreal. But the feeling that was upon me—enveloping, permeating, thrusting me to the edge of timelessness and spacelessness—was powerful, substantial, and in every way gleaming with Reality.

The feeling enveloped me and departed quickly. It probably consumed less than 30 seconds of time. It didn't coincide with any knowledge I had acquired up to that point, nor with any that I was to encounter for nearly ten more years. I wondered about it occasionally, but like so many who have had a mystical experience, did no further investigating. I've regretted that lapse ever since.

If inner promptings similar to those poetically described by Tennyson, or to the questions I've asked in the first paragraph, or to the personal experience I've described— if such inner promptings hauntingly intrude upon your consciousness from time to time, you are indeed ready for the Great Journey. With very few necessary preliminaries, then, we will set forth upon the Path.

Let's look again at Tennyson's poem. It offers the essence of mysticism, whether from an experiential or doctrinal point of view. It says that Something, which seems almost as a dream to the normal consciousness, really exists around you, within you, everywhere. It's dreamlike, yet it's real. It's out there, yet it's in here. It moves and acts and you can feel it, yet your fingers cannot touch it. It takes shape, but is formless. It is visible, but cannot be described. As a matter of fact, it's like being in love. If you've ever loved deeply, you know that you cannot describe it. You feel it, yet it's much more than a mere feeling.

The mystic seeks that indefinite and misty Nothing-Everything. "If it's so vaporous," you may ask, "how do I know it's there?" The answer is that if it didn't exist, you wouldn't seek it. A sage once said, "You cannot hunger for a food you've never tasted." The spirit hungers for the Spirit.

If, in some vague area of your consciousness, the mystic gleam of the Grand Reality has left a spark of light, it calls you now. "Follow Me," it says, and those words have the same magnetic attraction and irresistibility they did when spoken by saviours, prophets and avatars—by the Sea of Galilee, in the Wilderness of Paran, on a Himalayan mountain, or wherever an aspect of Reality has become focalized in a superior human being.

In her classical definition of mysticism, Evelyn Underhill has described it as the art of union with Reality. She further describes a mystic as a person who has attained that union to some degree, greater or less, or a person who believes in and strives for such attainment.

The highest Reality of which humankind has been able to conceive is God. But who or what is God? If you are going to find union with that Reality, you need to know, insofar as you can, what that Reality is. Tennyson, in his poem, poetically projects a goal. I prosaically propose a method to reach it.

The first step is to know what you are striving for.

The second is to know where it is located.

And the third is to know how to get there.

We begin with our goal, the highest Reality of which we can conceive—God. (I respectfully ask my Buddhist friends to read Nirvana in place of God.) Ask anyone, even yourself, who or what God is, and you won't get a very satisfactory answer. You will receive different answers at different times from the same person and, obviously, different answers from different individuals. Your own answer will vary from time to time. What this means is that in your normal level of consciousness you are apprehending different aspects of the Infinite depending upon the conditions of the moment.

Would it not be easier to achieve a degree of union with God if you could be more definite and less variable about your concept of that Highest Reality? Of course, for then you would have a better idea of your goal. How can there be an affirmative answer to the question, "God—are you really there?" if you haven't a pretty definite conviction of who or what you are talking to?

So, to take our first step, we will examine some of the ways to conceive of God. They will not be exactly the same for any two persons. You aren't required to accept the discernment of God which appeals to me, nor I to accept that which appeals to you. After we've examined these possibilities, I'll help you organize and tabulate your own observations. Then you will know with a fair degree of exactness the nature of the Reality with which you seek to unite.

Swami Parampanthi, author of *Creative Self-Transformation*, (published by Astara, Upland, Calif.; 1974), a meditation instruction book, once made a statement which I frequently recall as a guide to my own activities—"Think of the fortunate person who knows where he is going." You can be that fortunate person here at the beginning of the Inner Journey, the most important journey you will ever undertake.

Let us create the setting in which you may acquire that kind of fortunate knowledge. Let us get to know your concept of the precise form and nature of the Highest Reality which is your goal. We will do it by considering the several ways in which humankind has pictured the Infinite Being through all of time, and sought through those imperfect vehicles of spiritual aspiration which have been termed "religion."

Here, then, is the first of several guideline ideas which may help you relate to Reality. You will see your personal goal much clearer after you have considered and either accepted or rejected, or accepted with reservations, one or more of these ideas about God. Your concept of God conditions the kind of mystical experience you are most apt to encounter.

> God as a Person
> God as Love
> God as Intelligence
> God as Energy
> God as Cosmic Consciousness
> God as Light
> God as Spirit

GOD AS A PERSON

Countless individuals in every religion known to humankind see God only as a Person. They look for God from a physical-level viewpoint. I do not imply any criticism when I suggest that this is a primitive approach. Nor do I suggest that perfectly valid mystical experiences are not possible in the lives of those who share this view, for they do occur.

I think it is well, however, for us to recall that the word

persona, from which the word *person* is derived, means an actor's mask, something which hides the real identity of the one who wears it.

Think of someone you know. That individual is a person. But, looking at that person, you see only a mask of the true individual. The physical-level viewpoint gives you limited information. You must use other forms of perception and analysis to penetrate the mask and arrive at a clearer realization of what the individual truly is.

Perhaps, then, you would like to consider that in looking at God as a Person, one sees a mask which hides other qualities of the Infinite Being, qualities more meaningful and to which one may more easily become attuned.

GOD AS LOVE

From a physical-level view of God as a Person, we progress to the emotional-level view of God as Love.

"The Lord is my shepherd," said the Psalmist. In metaphysical symbology, animals are said to represent the emotional nature. And in most animals which are to the slightest degree domesticated, the relationship is usually one of pure love. To the Psalmist, the relationship between shepherd and flock exemplified the expression of love flowing in two directions.

From flock to shepherd: a purely emotional love, devoid entirely of any higher thought process.

From shepherd to flock: an emotional love carried to a higher degree by the addition of thoughtful attention in the form of protection, providing food, shelter and other considerations.

To say that God is Love is an emotional-level view of the Infinite Being, but not from the standpoint of morbidness, hysteria or maudlin sentimentality. It is a higher and truly unitive type of emotion, which has been experienced by the great mystics through all of time.

"God so loved the world," says the Gospel of John, "that he gave his only begotten Son . . . ." In the days of that Gospel the father-son relationship represented the highest kind of emotional tie. Therefore, no act could exemplify the emotion of love to a greater degree than offering one's son on behalf of other persons or for an ideal. In this instance, it was deemed to be both.

"God is love," says the First Epistle of John, "and he that dwelleth in love dwelleth in God, and God in him." One might say that for many persons that sentence contains all the information necessary for attaining the Mystic Union. Providing, of course, that it is not a selfish love expressed purely for the gratification of one's own desires. If it is *outgoing love,* then it fulfills the spiritual requirements, and union with God may result.

GOD AS INTELLIGENCE

Many persons find the orientation of their lives on the mental level rather than the physical or emotional. This does not mean they are superior, nor does it mean that those who love do not think. It is simply to pinpoint a predominant level of individual mind-set.

Just as there are snares on the physical and emotional levels, so is it true on the level of intelligence. Pride and arrogance are the chief offenders. The unknown author of the Book of Samuel pointed this out as he warned against entertaining those characteristics in one's consciousness. Then he added, ". . . the Lord is a God of Knowledge . . ."

It is possible to find the mystic union through the intellect. It requires acceptance of the idea that God is *the* center of Intelligence. Man is also a center of intelligence, subsidiary to the God center and functioning within it.

"How can anyone think of God as Intelligence?" someone may ask.

If you have ever suddenly solved a puzzling situation—one that seemed hopeless before its dramatic solution—you may recall the feeling of exhilaration and upliftment that flooded your being. That feeling is akin to the sensation of oneness which may be experienced by those who think of God as Intelligence.

GOD AS ENERGY

In considering God as Energy one does not think of blind, undirected power, but rather as a kind of dynamism which permeates the universe—an energetic, living Presence.

This Presence animates humankind as described symbolically in the Bible: "And the Lord God formed man of the dust of the ground and breathed into his nostrils the breath of Life and man became a living soul."

The Presence animates not only human life but all life, everywhere. It animates, with differing degrees, life in the various kingdoms—mineral, vegetable, animal and human.

As with all concepts of the Infinite, God as Energy or Force cannot be fully known and remains, in part, a mystery. It was Job who asked, ". . . the thunder of His power, who can understand?"

GOD AS COSMIC CONSCIOUSNESS

Many mystics have experienced flashes of Cosmic Consciousness. In most instances, though not always, it occurs during a period of meditation or deep relaxation or an almost self-hypnotic state of reverie.

The experience of Cosmic Consciousness is the highest aspect of several simultaneously occurring phenomena and inner sensations. There is a sudden appearance of brilliant light in and through one's being. There is a sense of buoyancy as though released from a heavy burden. Every physical sense sitmulus relating one to immediate surroundings disappears. There is a deepening sense of reality and the realization that, for an ecstatic moment, all knowledge and wisdom—Cosmic Consciousness—is resident in your consciousness.

GOD AS LIGHT

Can you imagine light which is animate and possesses an indefinable quality of personality?

It is the experience of sensing such a phenomenon which leads many to refer to God as a Being of Light.

Symbolically, light indicates wisdom, understanding, emergence from darkness or ignorance, initiation to a higher status of spiritual accomplishment. "I've seen the light," is a phrase which may be applied to any situation from the ridiculous to the sublime. The total scope of light as a symbol gives it deeper significance as representative of God.

Modern science tells us that the brain, as a sensory instrument, can detect light even though the eyes are blind.

If this is true of the brain on the physical level, is it not possible that on the spiritual level the consciousness, as a higher sensory device, can perceive God as Light?

The inner sensing of the Divine Personality as Light may very well be what John referred to in his Epistle when he said ". . . God is Light and in Him is no darkness at all . . . ."

GOD AS SPIRIT

"God is Spirit . . ." says John in the Fourth Chapter of his Gospel. God is the kind of Spirit that is omnipresent, omniscient, omnipotent, eternal, infinite.

"God created man in His own image." Therefore man is spirit also, possessing the same qualities found in God, but centered on a different vibratory level. It is inconceivable that the life essence focalized in an individual be drastically different than its Source, just as a drop of water must contain the properties and characteristics of the ocean from which it is removed.

God is Spirit. They that worship Him ". . . shall worship the Father in spirit and in truth . . . ." Personally, I cannot imagine the Infinite Spirit wanting me to prostrate myself eternally in a state of worship. But I can imagine the Infinite Spirit being most ready indeed to interact with me.

A friend once paved the way for me to obtain a position with a large company. "How can I show my appreciation?" I asked. "By doing a good job," he replied. He wanted no adulation from me. Nor does God. I think the word *worship* means *interact*.

Let's paraphrase the scripture in that way. *God is Spirit, and they that interact with Him must interact in spirit and truth.*

How do we interact with God? It is a mystical experience in which your spirit and the Infinite Spirit intercommunicate on a vibratory level common to both. You will find various ways for this to occur throughout the pages of this book, especially in the Self-Discovery Guides which conclude each chapter.

How do you think of God? What characteristics inherent in the Great Personality are most meaningful to you? It is helpful to decide, even though next month you may change your view.

Everyone's name for God, everyone's description of God, everyone's analysis of God is valid. Never feel that your view is unacceptable. Obviously, if God is Everything, then God is included in every description. God is simply described and known on different levels according to the level of understanding and acceptance which the describer and knower has attained.

One level or another is not necessarily superior or inferior. Each is simply more meaningful, more helpful, more acceptable to *you* at a given moment. The nature of your life expression varies from one point in time to another. Those points might be separated by as long a period as many years, or as short as a few minutes. Almost instinctively you turn to those aspects of the Infinite most essential to your needs.

You are therefore wise to consider that the way you view God illumines, to some degree, the path of your own life experience and your very personal needs along that path. Further, it gives insight into your purpose for incarnation and the nature of the magnetic "pull" between you and the greater dimensions of life. It reveals to your normal level of consciousness something of the current activity in a superior level of your consciousness, sometimes referred to as the High Self—that aspect of your being which functions nearest life's spiritual octave.

The affinity of similarities between you and the Infinite Being help draw you into experiences of interaction, one with the other. Self-Discovery Guide I, which follows, will help you learn more about the aspects of God for which you have a natural inclination. Then in the next chapter we will look into those aspects of *your* being for which God has an affinity. In the Third Chapter we will put the similarities together to improve interactive experiences.

*   *   *   *   *

Mysticism is the human, direct way to God.

*   *   *   *   *

SELF-DISCOVERY GUIDE I

This is the first in a series of guideline ideas to be offered with each chapter of this book. The guideline ideas, called Self-Discovery Guides, are designed to help you experience the mystical occurrence which each chapter discusses.

Ultimate Reality, God, is the subject of Chapter 1. It is said that "man cannot know God," yet every mystic has experienced sublime moments of union with the Infinite. The attempt to know God to some degree at least is well worthwhile, and leads to further experience of union with Reality.

Mysticism is the art of union with Reality. How do you practice that art?

Your starting point is your present conscious understanding of God. You may say that you cannot put it in words but you can. Imagine that someone you love is at this moment experiencing an emergency and you wish to seek help for that person through prayer. To whom or what do you address the prayer? Your answer to the question describes your concept of God at this moment, your starting point.

You will come to have a deeper sense of God by determining which aspects of the Infinite Being you consider most meaningful, most magnetic. To help you make this determination I offer an alphabetical list from which to make choices. It is far from complete and you may wish to make a number of your own additions.

Select the four or five aspects which most attract you. Then, in a daily moment of inner attunement, begin your meditation by centering your consciousness on one of those aspects. Remember, only one aspect during each meditation period.

Follow through with meditation on the other aspects which appeal to you until you begin to formulate a close, personal relationship with the Infinite Being. In the Book of Job we read, "*Acquaint now thyself with Him and be at peace.*"

GOD AS . . .

Builder	Healer	Provider
Chastiser	Intelligence	Redeemer
Companion	Infinite Being	Refuge
Compassion	Joy	Shepherd
Confidant	Judge	Spirit
Cosmic Consciousness	Kindness	Strength
Co-Worker	King	Sustainer
Creator	Light	Sympathy
Deliverer	Love	Teacher
Divine Mind	Mercy	Truth
Energy	Mother	Understanding
Father	Omnipotence	Universal Space
Father-Mother	Omnipresence	Wisdom
Force	Omniscience	——————
Friend	Partner	——————
Goodness	Perfection	——————
Guide	Power	——————

*   *   *   *   *

Chapter 2

SELF—WHAT ARE YOU DOING NOW?

Once I was riding in a jet about seven miles high on an especially clear day when the pilot called attention to a lake in a volcano crater nearly 150 miles away. It's a thrill to be able to see that distance. "But then," I thought, "how puny it really is when compared to the distance an astronaut can see."

Let's put ourselves in an astronaut's space capsule. He can see ten thousand times further than we can. But, in turn, he must also say to himself, "As much as is visible, I really see very little of all there is in the universe."

There's an analogy here between seeing at a distance and looking at your Self. Undoubtedly you catch occasional glimpses of your true being, beyond your normal conscious personality, as I had my glimpse of the distant lake. Perhaps you may on rarer occasions see a still further extension of your Self just as the astronaut sees more than the earthbound.

But, however much of your Self you may consciously know, it is only a fraction of your total being. Your Self may have its center at one point in space, but its range is the universe. In a writing called *Space Time*, Ralph Waldo Emerson pointed out that present in every person—in you and me—"is the sum of all things past" as well as the potentials for all "the years that yet remain," and he went on to say that the Self, in a kind of slumbering way, contains the ability to reach to the highest heaven as well as to achieve every "accomplishment Divine."

In light of this statement, which merely hints at the combustible possibilities inherent in the expanded consciousness, you might begin the awakening of that vast slumbering portion of your being by directing a few questions to it. The first could well be, "Self—what are you doing now?"

"For one thing," your Self will reply, "I'm gathering information and incorporating it into the inner library of knowledge I've acquired through the ages."

"What do you do with this knowledge?"

"Little by little, I try to filter whatever is needed into your normal level of consciousness, the level that is questioning me now."

"Then why am I not more intelligent than I seem to be?" you ask.

"You *are* more intelligent than you seem to be. It is only that keeping your attention almost exclusively centered on activities of the everyday world creates a barrier between my range of your consciousness and your normally functioning range.

"So, I accomplish more than you realize, especially when you are asleep, for then the connection between your body and your normal consciousness is neither as binding nor as limiting."

"Self-what else do you do?"

"I seek ways to express talents and fulfill obligations previously acquired, and I inspire your normal consciousness to acquire new talents as well as improve old ones."

Now at this point you have several choices to consider. First you should decide whether or not you think I've lost my senses for writing such a conversation as you've just read. If you think I have, then close the book and put it aside forever—or until you are internally prompted to read it again. You see, any person who accepts mysticism as a way of life should also be prepared to be judged mentally unstable. More on this point in a moment.

Your next choice is to decide whether or not a conversation such as I've described could possibly occur. If you're in doubt, I suggest that you try it a time or so. Be alone; become quiet; ask the same questions or think of others. See if answers in the form of impressions really do enter the perceptive gate of your normal consciousness. If any subtle intuitions do appear, make notes of them for further consideration later. You may very well be surprised at the personal enlightenment you gain during the process of speaking with your Self.

It is a way to do what Wordsworth must have been thinking when he said, "By all means sometimes be alone; salute thyself; see what thy soul doth wear; dare to look in thy chest, and tumble up and down what thou findest there."

But what about people who talk to themselves or who talk to God or to animals or plants? Aren't they a little strange? Aren't they victims of some neurosis or psychosis?

There are many, of course, who believe this to be true. There are those who insist that Jesus, Moses, Buddha, Mohammed and every other saint and sage, all suffered from a hallucinatory consciousness, or from ego-mania, or a martyr complex, or any one or a combination of several types of inner instability. Obviously the great traditional mystics did not conduct or express themselves in a manner that would be considered normal for most of us.

If I were living with certain members of my family during the time of Jesus there might have been a conversation such as this at an evening dinner. I would begin by saying:

"Uncle Wendell, I was at the well today and watched Jesus heal a crippled man. Then he told a woman all about her past and future. You should have been there!"

"My boy, I've been a scientist and university professor for years, and I assure you that fellow has all kinds of hallucinations and he has a lot of fools hypnotized into believing in him. Stay away from him for your own good."

"But uncle, he says he is in God and God is in him."

"You see! He's also an ego-maniac!"

You can easily imagine a similar conversation with someone in your family about any of the avatars, saviours, or sages you revere. They indeed may be thought of as neurotic or psychotic, if what your champions think or do, appear to hear or see, are considered as symptoms, rather than as legitimate functions. But why should other than normal behaviour necessarily be considered as symptomatic of grevious ills? Can it not equally be thought of as the expression of genius?

The inventor type of genius, or the business genius, or the architectural, medical, legal or any other kind of genius exhibit the same symptoms as the spiritual genius. The symptoms are merely directed toward a different end and measured by a different yardstick.

It is interesting to note the relationship between the neurotic temperament and the religious. William James, in *The Varieties of Religious Experience,* (published by Dolphin Books, Garden City, New York; Doubleday & Co., Inc.) devotes the very first chapter to it, under the title, *Religion and Neurology.* Because I've always had a non-scientific interest in the mind, I've re-read this chapter a number of times, perhaps in part because I delight in his beautiful lampoon of diagnosis with the statement: "Medical materialism finishes up Saint Paul by calling his vision on the road to Damascus a discharging lesion of the occipital cortex, he being an epileptic."

So if you consider yourself a mystic (as I do) and worry about what your friends think of you (which I once did but do no longer), take comfort in the fact that the symptoms you display place you in good company—although admittedly it is company made respectable by passing centuries.

WHAT THE GENIUS, NEUROTIC AND MYSTIC SHARE

Perhaps you will be heartened by a brief comparison of characteristics common to the genius, the neurotic and the mystic. First, all three are capable of the most *intense thought*. To them, thought becomes almost akin to the laser beam in science, a concentration of light elements resulting in remarkable powers.

Beginners in meditation practices often discover to their dismay that the mind remains centered on a thought only for a few brief seconds, then it leaps to another. The Hindu calls this the "monkey mind," constantly leaping from thought to thought as the monkey jumps from branch to branch. The genius, the neurotic, the mystic, the practiced meditator, have developed control of the mind enabling them to hold it steadfastly on a subject with tremendous intensity.

Next, all three—genius, neurotic and mystic—generate a profound *depth of interest* in any subject which attracts their attention.

It is possible to think intensely, though superficially. Depth of interest is another matter. The mind of such a person is like a bottomless well. No matter how much of a subject comes to his attention, the mind is never satisfied and constantly seeks more. Accompanying it is a kind of exclusivity of thought. It becomes possible to exclude extraneous matter almost as though it didn't exist, so the depth of interest is an unhindered exploration of a subject in its every facet.

A third denominator common to our three "strange" groups is the matter of *individuality*. They do not think in the same patterns as do the multitudes. Ideas which the "normal" person would consider totally incompatible are put together in perfect harmony. By this process a superior invention comes into the view of the genius, the neurotic satisfies himself with a concept which is totally inconceivable to the rest of us, the mystic originates a new way of viewing Reality which may in time even become one of the world's great religions.

The final point of comparison between genius, neurotic and mystic is that each bears upon his mind the indelible stamp of *receptivity to the mystical*. The genius is open-minded about the secrets hidden in his field of interest. To the neurotic, almost everything has its hidden meaning which only he perceives. And the mystic gives his name to it all.

DOORS OF PERCEPTION FOR THE MYSTIC

To the mystic, the five obvious physical senses—seeing, hearing, feeling, smelling and tasting—are the lowest and most primitive of perceptors, "doors of perception" for the physical-level world only. Nevertheless, in order for the Self to express in the best possible fashion, and to aid in the process of bringing higher senses into play, it is important to cleanse or purify the physical senses. How is it accomplished? How do we sweep away the debris which clutters the clear path of the Self and prohibits its full expression through the being which you are?

To the traditional mystic, the first consideration is always the *practice of morality*. It is difficult to state the relationship between morality and mystical expression. Morality differs in every culture. For some reason the acceptance of a moral code, and the practice of that code, is related to having mystical experiences.

The unprincipled person according to the standards of his culture, whatever they may be, is more predominately oriented to the physical senses and more apt to discredit and have no personal interest in anything beyond those senses. This negative attitude of mind is an extremely limiting factor which closes more firmly the doors of perception instead of opening them.

A second door of perception is *inspiration*. Most of us are rather vague about what inspires us and go to inspirational sources on a rather haphazard basis.

"What inspires me?" is a question you should ask yourself frequently the next few days. Then, if possible, assemble your sources of inspiration for ready availability. Are you inspired by music, literature, scriptures? Keep all your inspirational material in one place in your home so you may go to it quickly and as frequently as you wish. Its use will be emotionally and psychologically cleansing as well as helping clear the way to the higher senses.

We frequently fall into the trap of mistaking entertainment for inspiration. Entertainment is important to your life, and at times you may be entertained and inspired simultaneously. However, normally the objectives of each differ. Make certain you distinguish between the inspirational and entertainment values of your material.

Physiological, psychological and environmental cleansing are important to the mystical experience. It is possible for an individual to live in unclean surroundings and still experience mystical phenomena. The prodigal son had an awakening while living in the field with the swine. Individuals have encountered Reality in jungles and jails, tenements and tents. But the obscure relationship of physiological, psychological and environmental cleanliness with the mystical experience prevails in most of our lives. If we cannot actually go to the clean, pure, invigorating mountain, we can help bring the mountain to ourselves.

". . . he that hath clean hands shall be stronger and stronger," said Job.

"Who shall ascend into the hill of the Lord, or who shall stand in his holy place?" asked the Psalmist, and immediately answered, "He that hath clean hands, and a pure heart; who hath not lifted up his soul unto vanity, nor sworn deceitfully."

And later, "Create in me a clean heart, Oh God; and renew a right spirit within me."

Symbolical Cleansing is an aspect of psychological cleansing that deserves attention. Minds and emotions are often freed of accumulated litter by certain physical acts (such as church attendance, visualizing a religious symbol, meditating in a shrine).

At Astara we often use the phrase, "I am surrounded by

the pure white light of the Christ." Light has long been a symbol of cleanliness. And who is to say but that mentally visualizing light actually does create a kind of ultrasonic solvent for cleansing the physical, emotional and mental self just as industry cleans with ultrasound.

I often wonder, as I visualize myself surrounded and permeated by the light, "By this process am I not unburdening the atomic structure of my being of some of the obstructions accumulated through life in this processed food, negative news, hurry up and wait world in which we live?"

The answer that comes to me is in the affirmative. So psychologically, if not actually (though I believe the latter), there is a bonafide and beneficial response in me.

Simplification is another kind of broom with which you can sweep away inner debris. Ideas about mystical experiences, and methods for attaining them, are frequently very complex. You may be one of those persons for whom the act of simplification itself is mystically cleansing and exhilarating.

Orderliness is still another tool which aids the inner purifying process. I've known many persons who lived cluttered lives. They may have been tremendously interested in mystical matters, but mystical experience was more often than not denied them. Orderliness helps create the receptive inner simplicity which not only invites mystical experience to enter but also holds wide the door.

It is of course possible to ignore any of these methods and still experience the sublimity of union with the Infinite. Paying attention to them is merely a matter of personal interest. They are given not because they are imperative to the process but because they help.

The principle method remains the traditional one of

meditation. In one form or another it is found in every culture known to humankind. There are nearly as many meditation methods as there are teachers.

Basically, meditation is the practice of stilling the outer self so that deeper and higher aspects of your being come into focus and expression. Whatever method becomes your favorite, remember it is best to enter any meditation session with a specific objective in mind. Your special interest during a single session might include any of the following but should be limited to one objective only:

1. The simple attainment of a momentary state of reverie.
2. To gain a state of physical and/or emotional well-being.
3. To stimulate mental alertness, creativity, etc.
4. To foster the expression of intuition or other psychic abilities.
5. To reach a state of ecstasy.
6. To approach and ultimately attain Illumination.
7. To arrive at a realization of Oneness with Reality.

"A child needs love the most when it is least deserved," is a saying I came upon many years ago. Through the years I've come to realize there is no reason why that thought should be limited to children; it applies to all of us. It also has many corollaries; we can create one to apply to meditation: "That person most needs to meditate who is least interested in doing it."

Some individuals are psychologically so constituted that they cannot be physically, visually or audibly quiet and still more than a few seconds at a time. They suffer from a compulsive restlessness that takes its toll from their lives physically, emotionally and mentally. Once they become convinced of the benefits meditation provides, they are apt to force themselves into the discipline. The results are often unsatisfactory and they turn away then from an activity which could be of great benefit.

In the beginning, if you can be still no longer than 30 seconds, well and good. *Urge* yourself to gradually lengthen the time but do not *force* yourself. Meditate no longer than you are psychologically comfortable. As you continue the practice you will acquire the ability to be quiet longer and longer periods of time with a corresponding increase in benefits. How long? The average busy person (whatever that is) will meditate approximately ten to twenty minutes daily. Your personal preference, however, should be the only judge.

What should you gain in an inner personal sense from mystical experience? We can put together a composite picture by extracting ideas from the lives and teachings of the great mystics of the past, and from an objective observation of today's mystics.

FEATURES OF THE MYSTICAL CONSCIOUSNESS

There are identifying features which enable you to detect the strands of mysticism woven into the lives of others. By them you can determine the presence of the mystical consciousness, and can measure its quality, quantity and degree. Further, if you can be objective enough, and sufficiently straightforward in self-honesty, you can observe these features in yourself and with personal profit read a few pages in the book of your own life.

¶ LOVE. Look at a mystic and you will see love personified. The mystic doesn't say, "Look at me, I'm expressing love," nor even consciously think about it. The mystic simply expresses a love-impregnated phase of the life energy which passes through his being to the world, and asks nothing in return.

The mystic can love animals, plants, inanimate objects, ideas and ideals, as well as people, not with the desire to acquire, possess or manipulate but purely to express the bubbling well-spring of love that flows from his inner self.

¶ Joy. The mystic may be unhappy from time to time. Nevertheless there is a radiant quality which emanates from his being, needing no verbal expression of the fact that residing in this person is a bright rapture with life. There is a feeling of elation that frequently counterbalances and sometimes even seems to defy life's tragedies and sorrows.

¶ Peace. The mystic is a person of peace. He may of necessity engage in violent acts, but predominately he is oriented to a harmonious relationship with others, and with all of life for that matter.

This is not to say a mystic is by any means a completely passive person. The mystic will extend himself to his last breath if need be on behalf of his cause. History's pages reflect the glow of those who have done so.

¶ Perseverence. While peace and harmony are obvious strands in the fabric of the mystical life, that is no indication that the mystic is an insipid, servile person. Just as an athlete might strengthen his muscles with isometric exercises, the mystic would strengthen his consciousness through meeting the obstacles he encounters.

¶ Self-assurance. No arrogance. No strutting. No theatricals. In the mystic, reliance on the Infinite is often misinterpreted by others as indicative of a crutch on which an unsure self might lean. It simply isn't true. The mystic is a self-assured person. Turning regularly to higher dimensions is like adding carbon alloys to steel, making an already strong substance still stronger.

¶ A SENSE OF THE PRESENCE. An awareness of Something greater than himself or herself tints the consciousness of the mystic with a golden glow. Stated by inner feelings rather than specific words is the concept: "While I am an individual, self-directing atom in the body of God, a Greater Life constantly flows through me, a Greater Consciousness infiltrates mine.

"God has given me the franchise to establish a center of life here on this earth. Though the outward appearance seems to show that I am completely separate from the Infinite, it is not true. There are invisible, mysterious, and very helpful lines of communication and transmission by which Spirit and spirit are interlaced and blended in me."

THE JOURNEY OF THE SELF

There was a time, before your incarnation, when you existed on a higher dimension of life. In various unspoken ways your consciousness became inpregnated with the idea of incarnation on this physical level. At that time you began to accumulate the elements you wished to bring into incarnation with you. The process might be considered semi-automatic. In part it was natural, magnetic attraction, and in part the result of deliberation and discretionary judgment by you.

As the result of previous experiences, you may have decided that you wished to engage in certain specific endeavors. This is not to say that prior to birth you decided, "I'm going to be a bookkeeper." But through a combination of vibratory attractions and decisions in your own consciousness you outlined or programmed some of the basic areas in which you would later express yourself. You may have decided, for instance, I want to develop certain personality characteristics during this incarnation. Or, I want to express myself in certain ways.

With these various elements finally determined, either through natural selection processes or those of self-determination, you were finally ready for incarnation. At that point you were faced with the need to decide when, where and under what circumstances your incarnation was to occur. You had to select parents. Around the world there were persons in the process of creating physical bodies you could inhabit. What was it that determined you would incarnate in a physical body which would exist and express at the point in time and space where you were born?

Through a variety of circumstances—such a puzzle we could never put it all together, including the total lives of your parents, grandparents, etc.—you made a selection. At this point in your life you may or may not doubt the wisdom of your choice. There may have been many unhappy circumstances along the way, or a combination of happy and unhappy which is true of most of us.

But what was the origin of the physical body in which you were to have these experiences? We know that at one point in history the human body did not exist on earth. We know that at one time there were no living things at all. Somehow there was suddenly an amoeba—then two, then four, and they kept doubling in number and assuming different forms through mutations. In other words at a certain point there was an infusion of life into inanimate substance; the life was itself in the form of a pattern, and the substance assumed the patterned shape. Finally these shapes evolved into bodies that could serve the human spirit, and the spirit involved into them.

You incarnated through the parents of your choice in a body that was literally the result of a combined effort of several generations of thought processes (not merely sexual reproduction) plus your own magnetic pattern. During your physical lifetime you will acquire certain talents, learn certain lessons, express previously acquired talents and previously gained knowledge, and incur certain obligations.

At the close of your "day" on earth, you will gather your possessions—your accumulated talents, knowledge and obligations—and move to another mansion in the Father's House, one or probably a series of planes in the spiritual dimensions, and in time the process will begin again. However, it will not be a monotonous retracing of the same footsteps. Each round is a higher spiral on which the Self evolves in the spiritual range of life just as the body did (and still continues to do) in the physical range.

This brief synopsis of the journey of the Self is, obviously, not the belief of every mystic, particularly those who function within the boundaries of orthodox disciplines. However, it is a theme that is played over and over in the mystical symphonies of every culture. Whatever the orchestration, the melody is recognizable.

Are you, then, really immortal? Do you live beyond that momentary physical event called life?

As a mystic your inner monitor informs you of other levels of life on which your consciousness functions from time to time. Some of those levels are within the magnetic field of your own being; others extend into the "far countries" which are the spiritual homes of saints and saviours, the abodes of loved ones who have passed through physical life, the "place from whence you came."

In addition to intimations of immortality and the extension of life beyond purely physical dimensions, your inner monitor will from time to time tune in with mystical states which many refer to as "altered states of consciousness." That they are not normal is obvious. And they meet the requirements of William James' marks for classifying the mystical state: They cannot be fully described; they are mental, and not related to physical senses; they are transient, occurring then passing from the consciousness, never to be experienced again in exactly the same form (though very probably in similar forms); and finally, they usually (but not always) occur when you are in a passive mental phase.

"Self—what are you doing now?"

"I'm reaching for a more functional and productive state of cooperation with the Infinite."

That is what we seek in the next chapter.

It was an early mystic named Celsus who said, "If you close up the senses and look up with the mind, and if you turn from the flesh, and awaken the eye of the soul, thus, and thus only, shall you see God."

Taking his advice, then, though restructuring it to modern times, we shall now turn to the ways in which you and the Infinite may join to function harmoniously and productively.

*　*　*　*　*

Mysticism is an experiential awareness of Spirit.

*　*　*　*　*

SELF-DISCOVERY GUIDE II

Most persons spend a lifetime with their consciousness centered on themselves as purely physical beings. Many are at the point in their personal evolvement where they simply are not capable of any other awareness. But you are beyond that point, and I hope you are asking, "If there really is a self apart from the physical, how do I discover it?"

A starting point almost has to be the idea that consciousness conceivably could create a pattern on which a body might be built, but an inert mass of matter could hardly create a consciousness.

To acquire a deep-rooted awareness of one's spiritual self gives a non-egotistical sense of superiority and power over your body. It's a realization that body and spirit need each other for a time, can work together harmoniously and creatively—but that spirit and mind are captain and crew—the body is the ship.

One method for gaining awareness of your "higher identity" is through self-probing by self-questioning. A suggested plan is to select one question from the following list as a subject for intense contemplation and thought during quiet times. On another occasion select a different question. Add additional questions of your own. A result of this inner probing will be the emergence of a distinct feeling of self-awareness which temporarily excludes body awareness.

You are in the body, and body awareness is important, but of equal or even greater importance is occasional, or better still, regular recognition and realization of your spiritual self. So experiment with the self-answering technique, using these questions or your own, and note your progress toward discovery of Self.

1. Am I a purely physical being?
2. What causes personality differences? Genes and chromosomes inherited from parents? Or "shadings" of the incarnating spirit?
3. Are my emotions related to my body? Or to my mind?
4. Am I spirit?
5. Am I really part of the Being of God?
6. How long have I existed?
7. On a deep feeling level, have I ever really felt myself to be immortal? (If you have, or if you do during a future quiet time, review and re-experience the feeling several times.)
8. Have I lived on earth before? (If you feel you have, review the feeling several times without attempting to discover any details of a previous existence. Specifics are not important to this technique.)

In addition to self-questioning, the following technique may help you in your search for your self:

Be comfortably seated on a chair or sofa. Place any kind of object on a stand or table before you. Close your eyes and explore the object with your fingertips. Determine size, surface texture, shape. Remove your hands from the object and wait a few moments with your eyes still closed.

Do not physically touch the object again. Mentally direct your "spirit" arm, hand and fingers, to touch and explore the object as you previously did physically. Try to capture as definite a feeling of size, surface and shape as when your fingertips were in contact.

Experimenting with this technique a few times should confirm your awareness that your true being is something apart from your physical being, and cause your consciousness to function more frequently from its spiritual octave.

* * * * *

CHAPTER 3

YOU AND ME, GOD—WE'RE A PAIR!

"Of course we are. If you're Spirit, and I'm spirit, that makes us two of a kind. And if we have this common denominator between us, then there must be ways to discover and express it."

Learning these ways and using them constitutes a major portion of the mystic Path. Even the search itself is an adventure. Discoveries along the way are of a magnitude in personal significance which outshines even the most sensational finds of history's explorers. And those who think they have attained the ultimate still find unending frontiers in the ever-widening circles of their own consciousness.

Paul tells the Corinthians about it. "We speak the wisdom of God in a mystery," he says, "even the hidden wisdom . . . ." Then he discusses the fact that this wisdom is revealed by the Spirit of God, and that as the things of man can be truly known only by the spirit of man, so also can God be known only by knowing the Spirit of God.

"How can I bring Spirit and spirit together?" you might ask. "Where does the Divine meet the human in a knowable, functional relationship?"

Many would have us believe it happens automatically at eleven o'clock Sunday mornings in churches of the particular denomination where their memberships are held. You may wish to consider the idea that the only place God and man may meet is in God and man. It may occur at any time of day or night and at any place in the universe. "I am in the Father, and the Father is in me," not occasionally, but always.

Sometimes this infusion of Spirit with spirit occurs in apparently spontaneous instances. The written scriptures of all religions are saturated with such unexpected outpourings from Spirit to spirit. "The word of the Lord came to . . ." is the way many of the Old Testament prophets put it.

And thousands of family histories tell thrilling instances of spontaneous interactions between the Divine and the human paralleling the experience of Dr. Richard M. Bucke, described in his classic, *Cosmic Consciousness.* (Dutton Press, New York, N.Y.; 1970.)

He tells of falling into a state of reverie while riding home in a horse-drawn hansom following a social evening with friends. Suddenly he seemed to be engulfed in flames, accompanied by a state of spiritual consciousness which embraced superior knowledge and wisdom. Dr. Bucke's relaxed frame of mind, the rhythmic beat of the horse's hooves, the presence of light (the flame), are factors of import and we will return to them later. The point at the moment is that seemingly spontaneous occurrences are often the result of previous, controllable conditions.

So the mystical experience of interblending Spirit and spirit is not as haphazard or involuntary as it often seems. You may, in fact, cultivate it, invite it to occur, create the receptive conditions in which it transpires, and even control it to some degree.

Religious prophets may give us the word of God as they divine it, but they are not known for teaching *how* they receive the word. It has remained for the modern era to provide terminology and methodology, in response to the inquiring consciousness so prevalent in our age. Thus with each generation mysticism benefits from more knowledge, wider areas of acceptance, better ways of experimentation, and more and improved methods of instruction.

For example, to go back not too many years, Tennyson wrote to a friend stating, *"I have never had any revelations through anesthetics, but a kind of waking trance—this for lack of a better word—I have frequently had, quite up from boyhood, when I have been all alone. This has come upon me through repeating my own name to myself silently, till all at once, as it were, out of the intensity of the consciousness of individuality, individuality itself seemed to dissolve and fade away into boundless being, and this not a confused state but the clearest, the surest of the surest, utterly beyond words—where death was an almost laughable impossibility—the loss of personality (if so it were) seeming no extinction, but the only true life. I am ashamed of my feeble description. Have I not said the state is utterly beyond words?"*

Note that Tennyson describes a state in which spirit expands into Spirit . . . and Spirit infuses spirit. *This state always exists.* It becomes functional to a higher degree when awareness of its existence, and the possibilities inherent in its interaction, become activated in the individual consciousness.

By repeating his own name, "Tennyson . . . Tennyson . . . Tennyson . . ." over and over, the celebrated writer unknowingly (or perhaps knowingly) adopted the identical method of the Hindu sage who slowly chants, "Om . . . Om . . . Om . . ." for the same purpose.

There are unnumerable methods of activating the interactive qualities inherent in the fusion of Spirit and spirit.
Many of them will be listed and to some extent explored in
this chapter. You will be able to select and experiment with
those methods for which you have a personal affinity, and
thus make your way nearer the mother lode of spiritual
realization which bears many names, designated here as
Oneness with the Infinite.

"Yes, you and me, God—we're a pair!" And the next
step beyond that realization is described by Jesus in the
very mystical Coptic text, *The Gospel According to Thomas,*
(Henri-Charles Puech, et al., Harper & Row Publishers,
Inc., Scranton, PA; 1959), "When you make the two one,
and when you make the inner as the outer and the outer
as the inner and the above as the below . . . then shall
you enter (the Kingdom)."

So whether the mystical consciousness results from a
seemingly spontaneous incident, or is self-induced as the
result of deliberate disciplines and exercises, we must have
a beginning somewhere. An important beginning toward
a mystical experience is an examination of your thinking
and feeling about your relationship with the Infinite Being.
Use the following chart, not merely as a few words to be
read, but as a list of ideas to meditate on, and thus arrive
at your own personal feeling about your relation to the Infinite.

GOD IS:
A Parent—
    in some instances a Father, in others a Mother.
    Some religious traditions include a homogeneous
    Father-Mother God .

A King—
the Almighty, to be worshipped as a Royal Dignitary to whom utter obeisance is due.

A Judge—
the Presiding Officer of the Universal Court, making judgments, pronouncing sentences for sins, granting pardons for various reasons.

A Friend—
in some instances stable, in others of the "on again, off again" variety.

A Co-Worker—
whose energies parallel the efforts of the individual for the accomplishment of material and spiritual goals.

A Co-Creator—
whose motivation is toward assisting the individual to express the inner creative impulse in the arts, sciences, or as an individual person in any endeavor whatsoever.

As an exercise in attaining the mystical consciousness, copy the above list, add to it every description of the Infinite that you can conceive. (You may wish to make other selections from the list in the Self-Discovery Guide at the conclusion of Chapter One.) Then, over a period of many days, keep scanning the list while thinking, "Which of these is really meaningful to me in my relationship to the Infinite? Do I, each day, think of God as a Parent? As a Creator? What is the predominating relationship between myself and the Infinite?"

Keep your list at least a month. Each time you become aware of a specific type of inner relationship to the Infinite, put a check mark by it. At the end of a month, noting the descriptions followed by the largest number of marks, you'll

have an excellent outline—you might even call it a picture—
of your personal relationship with God. You'll know the
basis for the interaction of Spirit and spirit in your personal
life.

As important as the above exercise in consciousness may
be, it is really the foundation on which you build your relationship with the Infinite. There are numerous methods
for activating mystical experiences. We'll examine them
now. No one method is suggested as superior, for each person responds differently due to a host of factors. The methods are presented in brief form, the better enabling you to
pick and choose for you own continuing experiment, adap-
tation and practical use.

METHODS THAT LEAD TO MYSTICAL
ONENESS WITH THE INFINITE

¶ PERSONIFICATION OF GOD.   To realize the inner presence
of the Infinite or to have any kind of functional association
with the Infinite, it helps many persons to personify the Deity
—to picture the Infinite Being as a walking, talking Person with eyes and hands and other aspects of form identical to the human being.

The visual image thus created need not be correct in
order to achieve the desired result. For example, you may
read a news story about a person who is only a name to you.
If you visualize the individual, correctly or not, you heighten
your sense of empathy or inner feeling of oneness with him
or her. Carried to a sufficient degree, this process causes
psychological changes in your own being.

Therefore, personifying God as a Being is one way to

increase your empathy with the Infinite and is a valid method of achieving mystical oneness.

¶ FOOD. Mushrooms and peyote, soma and mistletoe, olive oil and honey, bread and wine—there is an almost endless list of foods to induce "intoxication" with the Divine, physiological or psychological, actual or hallucinatory. The custom has been universal to all cultures and times. Everywhere there is a "holy communion," a bread and wine, a physical substance ingested to attain a holy experience.

In contrast is the idea that, "It is not what enters into the mouth which defiles a man; but what comes out of the mouth, that is what defiles a man." (Matthew 15:11)

The mind rather than the stomach is the measure of the human being. But the wise person realizes that body and mind do interact. The better the body instrument, the more the mind can accomplish. The better the mind, the more proficient its instrument.

Jesus suggested the wine and wafer, which became the Rite of Holy Communion, as a mystical and symbolic way of inner attunement with him and his ideology. He was attaching significance not to a specific food as a method of spiritual realization but to the assimilation of that food with a specific thought uppermost in the consciousness.

He blessed the bread, gave thanks over the cup, and said, ". . . this do in remembrance of me." Not *to* remember me but *in* remembrance of me. The food was not meant to *cause* a spiritual experience; it was to pinpoint the idea that every level of being should *participate* in that experience. The intake of food, then, became a way to experience a mystical relationship with the Infinite through a memory association with the person who at that point in time and space was the supreme representative of the Infinite.

The "bread of life" is neither food nor person. To "eat" the bread is not the physical act of food consumption.

The bread of life is the spirit essence that emanates from God. To "eat" that "bread" is simply to assimilate it by making your consciousness compatible with it and then consciously to filter it throughout your being . . . your inner life and your outer.

¶ DRUGS. The use of drugs is closely related to food in attempts to induce the mystical experience. Is the use of drugs valid? Is the experience which results from drugs really mystical? Does it last? Are there non-mystical side effects?

There is difference of opinion, even controversy, about these questions. My opinion is that drugs should not be used as a method of achieving the mystical experience. There are a number of reasons.

First, we presume that the mystical experience is to lead us to a higher state of spirituality and purity. The intake of drugs immediately adds an impurity to the process.

For a second reason we look at the quite common statement of medical science that "drugs do not heal." And if they cannot heal, how can they confer spirituality?

The mystic attempts to develop the psychic centers. Drugs disrupt and uncontrollably stimulate those centers.

Drugs destroy the body's communication centers. Simple aspirin, for example, doesn't really stop your headache, it merely dulls your awareness of the pain. The mystic wishes the awareness sharpened to the highest possible degree rather than have it dulled to the point of total numbness.

Drugs do produce unusual experiences. But there is a considerable distinction between an unusual *experience* in consciousness and a mystical or exalted *state* of consciousness. Drunkenness is an unusual experience in consciousness but not an exalted state. An unusual experience in consciousness is the child of a few transitory moments. It is short-lived. A mystical or exalted state of consciousness is the result of a residual spiritual quality which is forever surfacing in varying degrees. It is everlasting.

¶ PRAYER.   In all religions and at all times prayer has been a traditional door to the mystical experience. "Pray without ceasing," wrote Paul to the Thessalonians.

Jesus told his followers that prayer is a personal, intimate and secret matter. From his instructions it is obvious that he believed the process of prayer to be highly mystical. Here is a condensed list of his instructions about prayer, followed by my comments.

. . . *enter into thy closet* . . . Center your attention upon the innermost depths of your own being. (Translating from the Aramaic, George Lamsa uses *inner chamber* in place of closet. Your personal inner chamber would be the head, heart, solar plexus, or whatever center you feel is the place where you meet God.)

. . . *And when thou hast shut thy door* . . . Through meditative disciplines close the physical senses or make them non-responsive to outer stimuli.

. . . *pray to thy Father which is in secret* . . . Become attuned with the God that is truly resident in your own Self (not the outer representation of God to which the unenlightened direct their attention).

It was after the above instruction that Jesus gave the words which have become known as *The Lord's Prayer*. It is preceded (See Matthew 6:9) by the words, "After *this manner* therefore pray ye . . ." The italics are mine because I believe he was not telling us to repeat the exact words, for he had just previously said, ". . . use not vain repetitions . . ."

I interpret the words, *Thy kingdom come* . . . to mean the inner state of mystical oneness with the Infinite. *Thy will be done in earth* . . . is meaningful to me in the sense that my physical body is the "earth" in which I am asking Divine Will to be expressed *as it is in heaven* . . . I seek the expression of Divine Will not as a total substitute for my own will but coincident with it, a harmonious functioning of one with the other.

"You and me, God—we're a pair."

The entire 17th Chapter of the Gospel of John is a prayer uttered by Jesus and filled with references to the mystical state.

"And this is life eternal, that they might know thee . . ."

". . . glorify thou me with thine own self with the glory I had with thee before the world was."

"And now come I to thee . . ."

". . . thou, Father, art in me, and I in thee . . ."

Here are statements of the truth of the mystical state, and a request that it be furthered, given in a poignant prayer on the eve of experiencing the machinations of total materialism, the betrayal by a friend for money. Certainly here is a stirring suggestion that the mystical state is a bulwark of personal strength during a time of trial. The entire chapter is discussing the association between spirit with a small "s" and Spirit with a capital "S."

¶ SCRIPTURES. Bernard of Clairvaux interpreted *The Song of Solomon* as describing the mystical union between Christ and the soul. It is but one instance in which a portion of a Holy Book is said to have a double meaning, saying one

thing in a literal sense and meaning another of metaphysical, mystical, or esoteric significance.

For many persons, reading and re-reading books of scripture create an inner atmosphere or state of exalted consciousness which can only be described as mystical. Words
become transmuted from the printed page into expanded,
exalted conditions of consciousness.

¶ BAPTISM.   The traditionally-minded Christian thinks of
baptism as immersion in water, or being sprinkled with it.
When you consider baptism as merely symbolic of tradition,
or at best as being cleansed in order to gain admission to a
group of the so-called "elect," then the superficial rite as
it is commonly conducted is satisfactory enough. But modern scholarship is substantiating the age-long claim of the
mystic that something more was intended.

"I indeed baptize you with water . . . but he that cometh
after me is mightier than I . . . he shall baptize with the
Holy Ghost and with fire," said John on the banks of the
Jordan. Obviously there were two kinds of baptism: one
was symbolic, the other an actual mystical experience.

Many now believe that the baptism which Jesus ad-
ministered was a very mystical rite, a kind of initiatory experience. The few who received it had first to prove their
worthiness. They received the rite only at night, dressed in
a symbolic robe, and isolated from the main body of followers. It was personal, intimate, experiential.

It's possible to receive this latter kind of baptism today,
either under the direction of a mystically inclined spiritual
teacher or entirely on one's own, as did Dr. Bucke. To know
the inner fire (the Hindu might term it raising the kundalini) is to receive the Holy Ghost, not in an emotional sense
but in terms of enlightenment.

¶ GLOSSOLALIA. "Mugawa afton tulanga oleimon fuldeva!"

If you heard those strange word-sounds pouring forcefully from the lips of one who normally spoke your language excellently, you would wonder at their meaning. Are they gibberish? We might pause a moment over the word *gibberish*, contemplating its possible significance in the practice of "speaking in tongues," or glossolalia as it is more formally known.

The word *gibberish* is derived from the name *Geber*—an alchemist of olden times who hid his formulas in strange words which he coined. Perhaps the words of one who speaks in tongues have no meaning except to hide the equally strange inner feeling of momentarily being one with Spirit. They seem not strange to the speaker, however unintelligible to the hearer.

The second chapter of the Book of Acts describes a meeting of the disciples made memorable first by strange sounds and sights (a "mighty wind" and "cloven tongues of fire"). Then they "began to speak with other tongues as the Spirit gave them utterance."

To those who encounter this particular path of mysticism it is life-changing, to say the least. One who has "gotten the Holy Ghost" is a different person. While it is usually induced in the company of many persons there are those who experience it while alone. There are Christian denominations in which it is considered the supreme experience, sublime and unexplainable.

¶ HOLY DAYS. Six of the holy days in Christianity are of prime importance for inducing mystical experience.

Christmas symbolizes the birth (and continuous rebirth) of the Christ Spirit in the individual, born in the cave of the physical form after being conceived by the higher consciousness of the individual.

Epiphany, celebrating the visit of the Wise Men, symbolizes the spirit of giving and the inner mystical feeling one senses as the result of giving or sharing.

Good Friday, the day Jesus was crucified and placed in the tomb, symbolizes more than a day of sorrow. It signals the use of introspection as preparation for still greater experiences to come.

Easter, the time of resurrection, illustrates liberation of the consciousness from the tomb of matter and elevation of the consciousness to a higher spiral of spiritual expression.

Ascension, forty days after Easter, signifies the completion of a mystical process—transmuting the physical body (begun at Easter) to a higher vibratory level compatible with the higher spiritual realms. It indicates that objects, situations, personalities, in fact all aspects of life and being, can be transmuted from one vibratory level of experience to a higher.

Pentecost, fifty days after Easter, speaking in tongues as overshadowed by the Holy Ghost, symbolizes the individual association with Spirit in an experiential way, sublimation of the normal self to Spirit.

¶ PILGRIMAGES — SHRINES. Jerusalem, Mecca, the Himalayas—the devotee of every religion makes his pilgrimage, whether around the corner to the community Sabbath service, or around the world to a sacred shrine.

During part of my boyhood I lived in Southern Ohio near a stream called Paint Creek. Indians of many tribes, even from hundreds of miles away, often the bitterest of enemies under normal circumstances, gathered there to find the paint stones which they dipped in animal grease and used to decorate their bodies. It was an unwritten law that no fighting would occur at the special place where the Great Spirit provided the ceremonial paint stones.

When near the banks of Paint Creek I always fancied I could sense the atmosphere of peace and harmony which enabled warring tribes to join in the common "fellowship of the search" for the stones which had spiritual significance for them. Now, in later years, I believe my feelings were much more reality than fancy.

Nearly every country has its shrines. Many people, of course, visit them for the purpose of receiving healing, either of illness or disharmonious circumstance. It is another experiential way of associating spirit with Spirit. If no other benefit is derived, there is at least the psychological sense of accomplishment at having made a journey.

Mystically, the pilgrimage is really the journey of the Self. It is the story of the prodigal son, out from his natural home into the world, learning the bitter lessons, and returning home to be accepted again into its better way of life. The Self leaves its natural residence place in the domain of Spirit, enters incarnation to learn many lessons, and finally returns to the higher dimensions again.

Making a pilgrimage, or visiting a shrine, is a kind of outer response to the inner desire to visit again the spiritual home from which the Self has been alienated during life on earth. It is the inner spiritual urge in action on the physical level.

It is an outcropping, too, of the "journey in consciousness" in its eternal quest to extend and expand and attain even higher goals. If you can divorce yourself from the tourism and commercialism which are too often interwoven into organized pilgrimages and visits to shrines, real benefits can be obtained. The process of sensing the spiritual realities often present in "holy places" may in fact be life-changing.

Every person is not affected in the same way by pilgrimages and shrines. First, of course, there is the matter of belief. One who does not believe is not apt to be as responsive as one who does. But there may be a deeper aspect. Can you see the possibility that each of us, in our own individual vibratory selves, has more compatibility with the vibratory atmosphere of one place than another?

Moses was told at the burning bush, ". . . put off thy shoes from off thy feet, for the place whereon thou standest is holy ground." Countless others at the same place beheld no burning bush nor received any such divine command. It was "holy ground" for him at that moment in time, that place in space, and in the existing circumstances. Mystically speaking, any place at any given moment may become a shrine.

¶ LIGHT.   In the *Gospel According to Thomas,* a Coptic text containing many sayings of Jesus, we read, "If they say to you, 'From where have you originated?' say to them, 'We have come from the light where the light has originated through itself. It stood and it revealed itself in their image.' "

The word *light* has long been meaningful in mysticism. "I've seen the light," is also a popular term meaning, "I've come to understand." The same phrase mystically signifies spiritual as well as intellectual comprehension. To be "in the light" is to express spiritual consciousness.

The spiritual Light is symbolized in many forms, from the brilliant sun to a feeble candle. "For the Lord God is a sun . . ." said the Psalmist. And one of Solomon's Proverbs states, "The spirit of man is the candle of the Lord."

The person who is mentally "held in the light" by another receives strength and protection in addition to his own efforts. And most every person who has had experience with meditation has encountered "the light" beyond description, either as an inward glow, a surrounding aura, or as an objective phenomenon.

¶ CRISIS. A powerful stimulant to a mystical experience is crisis—though it certainly is not one that I recommend. Thousands of lives are indebted to the pressures of circumstance which frequently force mystical psychic experiences into sharp focus in the consciousness.

One example is an incident in the life of John Barrymore, whose normal way of life would be considered anything but mystical. He had left his yacht, alone, to go hunting on a nearby island. While crossing a stream he stepped into quicksand and soon had sunk nearly to his waist.

Suddenly he heard a voice, which he recognized as his father's though the latter had long been dead. "Look up!" the voice commanded.

He did so, saw the overhanging branch of a tree which he was able to reach with his gun and pull toward him. Tugging on the branch gave him the additional leverage he needed to free himself.

Your newsstand offers several magazines and papers frequently featuring scores of similar incidents occurring daily, and thousands are never reported. Some such publications may present the totally sensational aspects, but they nevertheless have their basis in fact in the lives of the persons decribed.

¶ SYMBOLS. In casual conversation I occasionally ask, "What religious symbol is most meaningful to you? What symbol triggers a deep spiritual feeling?"

I was once surprised when a woman answered, "Geometrical designs."

"Geometrical designs in nature, or architecture, or paintings?" I asked.

"Anything drawn," she replied, "really moves me."

In Hinduism the *mandala* is a geometrical symbol, intricately drawn, and in many instances psychologically revealing of, or motivating to, the person who draws it. In fact, one of the traditional Hindu disciplines is for the student to draw a large mandala (a circular pattern of interweaving lines) and use it as an object of concentration during meditation.

Muslim temples are decorated with geometric patterns. A deliberate flaw in design is worked into each pattern— a misplaced tile, perhaps a broken line—in its own way a symbol of the idea that only Allah is perfect.

There is no question but that symmetry has a beauty that is uplifting. The lines of a cross, circle, triangle, square, and other symmetrical forms take on added significance to mystical responsiveness as you consciously associate them with personally meaningful spiritual ideas. They stimulate inwardly when used as objects of concentration, either casually or in moments of deep need, in the company of others or alone.

¶ HYPNOSIS.   In theatrical hypnotism, a subject usually is placed in more or less embarrassing situations before an audience and responds to the will of the hypnotist. The experience may be unusual but it is obviously not mystical.

In *The Secret Gospel of Mark* (Harper & Row, New York; 1973) Morton Smith suggests the possibility that Jesus used hypnotism during baptismal ceremonies he conducted (baptism with fire) to effect an especially deep connection between himself and the person receiving the rite. Jesus acted as the emissary of God, and through the ceremony the individual was brought into a state of unification with God—the goal of mysticism.

When you engage in meditation, you are more or less entering stages of self-induced hypnotism, stages in which you center conscious awareness less on the outer world, less on the self, and more on the inner world as it relates to the Spirit.

The tradition in the Ancient Wisdom is that the Hierophant placed the candidate for initiation in the mysteries into a state of hypnotic trance, placed himself in a similar state, then communicated the secrets of the initiation. This kept the secrets inviolate of course, for they could be neither seen nor heard by any eavesdropper. We might ask ourselves, "Was this what Jesus was doing during the course of his special type of baptism?"

¶ TRANCE. A second form of self-induced hypnotism is trance. The more psychic manifestation of trance is the type in which a discarnate spirit temporarily assumes control of the subject's body and speaks through it. In the more mystical manifestation the subject's normal consciousness is expanded and there is a total involvement of Spirit. The result is "feeling" and "knowing" on a much higher level during the course of the trance, with a trace residue of those qualities remaining in the normal consciousness afterwards.

¶ MUSIC. The kind of music that helps induce the mystical state in your consciousness depends upon the musical tastes you have cultivated. The Christian who lives in Los Angeles and the Christian whose home is Singapore will be influenced by different kinds of music. This is true even of different segments of the same nation.

The traditional Christian is mainly influenced by pipe organ music. The pipe organ dates back to the earliest known music. The original flute was very likely the tibia or leg bone, probably of a sheep. The "tibia" today is a term for a prominent organ voice producing an almost identical tone. Pipe organ tones (as different from electronic organ tones) are produced by air passing over the "lips" of pipes, just as air flows over vocal chords in the human voice box. Therefore the pipe organ comes closer to human vocal sound any any other mechanical instrument. There is even a pipe organ voice known as the Vox Humana, or human voice. Its tone approximates one of the vowel sounds, usually *ah* or *ee*.

Of course, many consider the most moving music to be choral, thus the choir is perhaps equally important with minister or liturgy in inducing the mystical experience; at least it should be.

Sounds that may not be musical melodies but simply tones in themselves, often help create mystical moments. I have a favorite Buddhist temple bell. Its clear, solitary tone soothes me and I occasionally just sit and listen to it, absorbing its vibratory tones into my being. I truly feel it helps align me with the cosmic elements with which I attempt to function in harmony.

In the stillness of one's being, a solitary sound affects the consciousness. I often sound the bell as I leave my office, and as I listen to the lingering tone till it dies away it seems almost an unspoken prayer, saying, "I am a vibratory Essence ready to go forth with you and sustain you in whatever you are attempting to do." Some—yes, many—will think me foolish. But then, my mystical consciousness has brought me to the point where I am little disturbed by what others think.

Perhaps the rhythmic clump of horses' hooves were a kind of music that helped induce Dr. Bucke's experience with cosmic consciousness. Modern tape and record players give us the opportunity to provide ourselves with any kind of music we wish for helping induce the mystical state of consciousness.

¶ SLEEP.   Is a dream a dream? Or is it an aspect of reality?

It can, of course, be either.

Do you leave your body during sleep, retaining your conscious awareness, to visit distant places on earth, centers of learning in the higher dimensions, deceased family members and friends?

It's all possible.

What are dreams? Symbols of significance welling up from your subconscious? Or communiques from your Higher Self to your normal consciousness?

They certainly can be either.

A word about the symbolic meaning of dreams. A symbol seen in a dream does not necessarily have precisely the same meaning for everyone. We have each woven into the fabric of consciousness slightly different meanings for the same symbol. A cross, for example, may symbolize either a burden or an aspiration.

Many years ago I dreamed of a rather bare room occupied by two tables. On one was the form of a lifeless baby. On the other was my father who had actually died some weeks prior to the dream. As I saw him in the dream he sat up, looked at me and smiled. The dream faded at that point.

Not long after the dream my wife, Earlyne, lost the child with which she had been pregnant at the time. The incident fulfilled my understanding of the dream—that no living being had been waiting to incarnate the baby form and be born into our family at that time—and further that my father had died only to this physical plane and was alive in the next dimension.

¶ NATURE. Nature is a powerful stimulant to mystical experience. Jonathan Edwards, an early American minister of tremendous influence, later separated from his congregation because of his non-traditional views (he became president of the University of New Jersey, now Princeton), told how a kind of trance-like state was induced in his consciousness when he went out into the fields of his father's estate and was surrounded by blue skies and green forests.

Views of nature—from the Grand Canyon to a tiny brook —can direct a current of the Divine into the consciousness and purify it sufficiently to be infused with Spirit.

¶ INCENSE. Among the major religions incense is important to a large portion of Christianity, Judiasm, Hinduism, and Buddhism. It's interesting to contemplate the fact that of the three gifts offered by the Wise Men to the Holy Babe, one was incense and another was perfume.

The olfactory sense is considered the most sensitive and powerful of the five physical senses. If strongly appealed to, it also makes the most indelible impression upon the memory. While in our everyday lives we normally apply it to mundane matters, there is no reason why it should not also have its spiritual significance.

Flowers at a shrine serve a greater purpose than beauty only. Their aroma is also spiritually stimulating. And symbolically it is their essence (which the aroma represents) which is the "offering" rather than merely petals, leaves and stems.

¶ TOUCH.   Can the sense of touch quicken the mystical consciousness?

The frenzy of fans to touch a sports hero, a political leader, or an entertainment idol illustrates the fact that an element of consciousness forcefully responds to tactile sensations. Touching the revered possession of an ancestor, the lover's touch, these are two additional illustrations of ways the consciousness replies to the language of contact.

In the mystical context, the "laying on of hands," whether for the purpose of healing, ordination or initiation, helps convey to the consciousness those qualities which engender its alignment with Spirit. In such instances the one who receives the touch benefits from the act.

In other instances the one who does the touching is the recipient of the altered consciousness and the resulting benefit. "If I may but touch his garment, I shall be whole," said the hemorrhaging woman. And so it was.

Ancient artifacts, lodestones, costly jewels or glass beads, the shark's tooth, the turtle's shell, the elephant's tusk, human bones or a lock of hair—these and thousands of other articles have been part and parcel of the mystical process, launched when fingers, forehead or chest come in contact with a revered object.

¶ IMAGINATION.   "Purely imaginary!" says the skeptic of mystical experiences. But he uses his own imagination as one of the intermediate steps to creative reality in his business, profession or other vocation.

Imagination isn't something that doesn't exist. It is. It's real. You wouldn't possess the faculty if there weren't a reason for it. Self-created imagery is one of humankind's most important psychological and creative tools, requiring no review here. When properly used it's a superior tool for activating the mystical state.

"Anything you can imagine is possible. What you can imagine yourself being, you can become." We are frequently offered these and similar statements in our everyday lives. They are no less true in the realm of mysticism.

The use of imagery (such as in visualizing yourself surrounded by a white, spiritual light) leads from the possible to the actual, from the unreal to the real.

When the paralytic is told, "Arise, and walk," it is a direct appeal to the faculty of imagination. He must overcome a lifetime of contrary patterns in the consciousness. He does it with the powerful imagery evoked at that moment. Out of spiritually centered imagination comes objective reality, in this instance in the form of physical healing.

¶ BREATH CONTROL. Traditional Christianity has had nothing to say about breath control being related to mystical states of consciousness. However, in the interchange between systems, Hinduism and Buddhism have offered scores of breath control disciplines which aid meditation practices of all kinds. The modern mystic in the Christian tradition borrows one or more of the many choices.

Just to sit quietly a few moments, while maintaining awareness of the breath rhythmically entering and leaving the nostrils, has a remarkable effect on the consciousness. To do this, or any other breathing exercise, with spiritual thought and objective, heightens the spiritual consciousness.

¶ INSPIRING EXAMPLES. The emulation of heroes, the inspiration of others who have achieved, propels the consciousness toward mystical areas of expression. We attempt what

Jesus has done, for he said, "As I have done so shall ye also do."

In our striving to fulfill these prophetic words there is kindled in us at least a degree of the divine fire so visible in him.

¶ SIZE. Some persons find that size prompts spiritual responses. The huge temple or synagogue is to some not merely more imposing but actually spiritually stimulating. On occasion, and in the right setting, a tiny drop of water may be more inspiring than the ocean.

¶ SINGLE WORDS. A "key" word often motivates the mind toward empathy with Spirit. "Hallelujah." "Shalom." "Om." These examples are from the Christian, Hebrew, and Hindu traditions.

However, the word used needn't be of religious significance. Tennyson repeated his last name. William James reported that for one person the word "chalcedony" had mystical connotations.

THE VALUE OF EXPECTANCY

In each of these methods for uniting spirit with Spirit, there is one ingredient that is the catalyst: Expectancy. The ancient alchemist would term it a universal solvent.

Job's oft-quoted words are, "For the thing which I greatly feared is come upon me, and that which I was afraid of is come unto me." His expectancy was fulfilled.

The value of expectancy in effecting the conscious union between spirit and Spirit is immeasurable. No expectancy— no union. "My experience occurred without my expecting it," is a frequent statement. But investigation usually reveals that expectancy was present in the background of consciousness, though quite possibly well disguised.

Following the *Self-Discovery Guide* we will examine ways you may interact with other than human forms of life, revealing a new dimension of your being.

*   *   *   *   *

Mysticism is a structure of mind in which the finite person becomes the active residence place of the Infinite Person.

*   *   *   *   *

SELF-DISCOVERY GUIDE III

"If expectancy is such an important ingredient for effecting the union between spirit and Spirit, how can I develop the quality?"

If you were going to plant a garden, you wouldn't toss the seeds out a second story window, letting them fall at random. Most persons generate expectancy just about as haphazardly. Remember first that expectancy might be defined as active faith. Then let's get a little organized about the particular kind of inner magnetic assurance you are going to generate.

Let's make a chart of all the different methods for prompting mystical experiences described in the preceding pages. Here's the list.

Method	1	2	3	4
Personification of God				
Food				
Prayer				
Scriptures				
Baptism				
Glossolalia				
Holy Days				
Pilgrimage—Shrine				
Light				

Method (cont.)	1	2	3	4
Symbols				
Hypnosis				
Trance				
Music				
Dreams				
Incense				
Touch				
Imagination				
Breath Control				
Inspiring Example				
Size				
Single Words				

Think about this list for awhile. "Which of these methods most appeals to me? If I am to arrive at some kind of experiential awareness of Spirit, by which of these methods, or combination of methods, shall I reach that goal? Which would I most like to use?"

Place a check mark in column one by each method you decide upon, no matter how many there may be.

Wait a week, then repeat the process, placing your check marks in column two. You may have changed your mind about some of the methods, dropping some, adding others.

Repeat the process two more weeks, using columns three and four. Examine carefully those methods which received the most checks. Circle them with colored ink or pencil. Or make a separate list of them.

Now the value of expectancy will begin functioning on your behalf. You've centered the focus of your expectancy on specific methods instead of allowing it to wander aimlessly. Your awareness is more open to activities in the areas you've selected.

Without this "pre-thought," a kind of selective tuning process, you are less apt to have the mystical experiences you desire. Concentration and self-preparation lead to the experiences whether they are deliberately entered into or are spontaneous and unexpected.

*   *   *   *   *

CHAPTER 4

THERE GOES THE BANANA TREE

Can a tree think? Is there consciousness in a stone?

I'll tell you a true story you may find hard to believe, though some who have heard it do not find it unusual for they've had similar experiences.

I was asked to speak to a group which I thought could appreciate mystical concepts. Late the night before, a little after midnight, I had mentally considered numerous ideas, but none of them appealed sufficiently. Wanting a little fresh air to help clear my mind I stepped out on the second story balcony of our home.

After a few deep breaths a momentary breeze rustled through the leaves and attracted my attention to a banana tree which at that time grew alongside the balcony. The top of the tree was a little higher than my head. I totally lost my concentration on the next day's lecture in the wild thoughts that suddenly swirled through my consciousness.

"I wonder what it's like to be a banana tree? If there's life there it must have sensations, and some element of consciousness. Does a banana tree think? If so, what does it think about?"

Without stopping to consider that all this was a little irrational, I mentally began to force my way into the tree. Not my body, of course, just my consciousness. I could feel mental energy building up around my head, and it spurred me on to still greater intensity of thought.

Suddenly—I was in the banana tree. Suddenly I *was* the banana tree! I knew that my physical self still stood on the balcony, leaning against the wall of the house. But *I* was in the tree and functioning with its consciousness.

I was disturbed about something. To put it in human terms, I felt two uneasy sensations—the sense of limitation, and the sense of frustration.

How long this lasted I have no idea. It may have been only a second—perhaps a minute or so. With a suddenness equal to the beginning of the experience I was myself again.

The next morning I decided for the first time to inspect the tree closely. As I approached it, the sense of limitation again came upon me. I suddenly realized the tree was indeed limited. It had neither the proper soil nor climate in which to express itself.

Then, as I stood under the tree, I looked up and was astonished to discover for the first time a tiny "hand" of bananas, the largest of which was smaller than my little finger! That explained the sense of frustration. The tree was capable of producing fine bananas, but was unable to do so.

Several years later the tree broke apart and fell. Its small roots simply couldn't hold up the weight of the large leaves.

"There goes the banana tree," was my sad thought, "and a little of me, too."

Each of us is expressing a type of differentiated life. We are separated from Universal Life as individuals. Most people never discover that there is a seamless robe into which each differentiated life is woven, the total weaving being Universal Life. Through the Universal Life each individual, each thread of separated life, becomes one with the whole and with one another. And this seamless robe is not limited to human life but also includes all other forms. Discovering the relationship between them constitutes part of the mystical process.

There is a passage in *The Gospel According to Thomas* which says, "Cleave a wood (a piece of wood), I am there; lift the stone and you will find Me there."

It seems to me that Jesus is saying that there is Universal Life and differentiated life, and the Christ Spirit is present in both. He may also be saying that life exists in seemingly lifeless inanimate things—a piece of wood or a stone.

Once when I told a friend about my experience with the banana tree he described a similar, and to me more astounding, experience. While walking on a mountainside he sat down to rest on a large rock. In a few moments he had the feeling of rapidly aging, then of feeling immobile and totally limited, as though tightly bound. Suddenly he realized he was not only on the rock, he was in it, with the same kind of penetrative and interlocking consciousness I experienced with the tree. One thread of the seamless robe touched strands with another.

Is there life in inanimate things? Although the tree from which it originated may have been felled many years ago, does a residue of life remain in its wood? Does something as physically dense and "lifeless" as a boulder on a mountainside "know" when you touch it? Once I wondered if we were cells in the body of God. Now I wonder if trees and dogs and fish and stones are too.

The differentiated, this-world consciousness in me says no.

The universal, mystical consciousness in me says yes—yes —yes.

Many so-called inanimate objects, and many living but not human objects, have their affinity with us—if not literally in consciousness then in symbolic and other motivating ways that contribute to the mystical sensibility.

An approach to the mystical is to remember that there is life everywhere, in the inanimate as well as the animate. Given the proper circumstances we can come in touch with that life. By that process we further our own understanding, our psychological and spiritual growth.

There are three aspects to other than human life that we will consider in a mystical context during the next several pages. Animals. Vegetation. Places and things. They affect your consciousness literally and symbolically.

ANIMALS

"Behold, I send you forth as sheep in the midst of wolves: be ye therefore wise as serpents and harmless as doves," said Jesus in a metaphorical mixture, suggesting that his apostles portray the qualities of sheep, serpents and doves. The symbolism is potent. What is its mystical meaning?

Much of the known world, prior to the life of Jesus, was peopled by shepherd kings and their subjects. Their kingdoms were small. Their principal form of wealth was sheep. With the passing years a new kind of shepherd came into existence. At the time of birth of Jesus we are told there were shepherds who became aware of the approach of messengers — from Spirit!—who told them of the event about to transpire. They were told where to go to participate in it.

These shepherds were not kings in the political sense of the word. They were shepherd *initiates* who were entitled to parts in the unfolding drama. Theirs was not material wealth, but spiritual worth. Their presence was needed in the process of focusing the Christ Spirit in its highest yet expression in physical form.

Mystical union is the focal point of the tenth chapter of John's Gospel. ". . . the Father is in me, and I in him." But leading up to that statement is a stream of esoteric comments regarding sheep, shepherds, *the* shepherd, the sheepfold and so on.

When Jesus mentions himself as the "door of the sheepfold" he is referring to initiatory experiences, as in the ancient Mystery Schools, with the hierophant (Jesus) introducing the candidates (the apostles) to that higher learning which cannot be given to the masses.

The apostles' consciousness was sufficiently spiritual and psychic to enable them to pass through the door into the sheepfold. In other words, they were qualified to receive the higher teachings and enter the company of the elect. Initiation through the "Christ process" leads to spiritual stature.

Metaphysically, sheep represent the emotions in a docile state, under control, as in a flock. So if you consider your emotions as a flock of sheep, and your consciousness as the shepherd, then it is by passing your emotions through the door of your enlightened consciousness that they too become enlightened, devoted to superior purposes, and make their contribution to your total being.

In the popular idiom, sheep are good and goats are bad, sheep are right and goats are wrong. Jesus used this symbology when he discussed the proper use of our talents and capabilities. ". . . separate them one from another, as a shepherd divideth his sheep from the goats. And he shall set the sheep on his right hand, but the goats on the left." He then stated that those on the right hand would inherit the kingdom.

How curious this idea of sheep on the right hand and goats on the left. The left half of the brain (the goat side?) is more oriented to action and materialism. The right half is concerned with spiritual, artistic, creative and meditative matters. Thus the sheep and goat segments of your own personality are separated according to the ancient tradition of the shepherd and his flock. Is this a key we will eventually be able to use by consciously directing thought through one side of the brain or the other, depending on our purposes and desires of the moment?

Other animal symbols also occur with frequency in the Scriptures. The dove, for example, is a harmless bird of peaceful disposition. Its voice is soft. It is not a predator. The white dove is a symbol of purity, peace and love.

At the time of Jesus' baptism a psychic light descended upon him. ". . . the heavens were opened unto him, and he saw the Spirit of God descending like a dove, and lighting upon him . . ."

The scene teems with symbolism as well as realism. To the traditionalist, it depicts a *gift* of the Spirit of God, exclusively conferred upon someone who was already divine. To the mystic it depicts a *response* by the Spirit of God to one who had achieved sufficient purity of purpose and degree of love to qualify for such an initiatory experience— and sufficient psychic ability to enable it to occur.

". . . I will make you fishers of men."

"Launch out into the deep, and let down your nets for a draught."

"Cast the net on the right side of the ship, and ye shall find."

Reference to fish appear with surprising frequency in the words and acts of Jesus. As the years passed, the symbol of the fish became a secret sign by which Christians recognized one another. It evolved into a sacred symbol through the Greek in which language the word for fish is an acronym for the phrase "Jesus Christ, Son of God, Saviour."

Because fish live in water (the symbol of mind) and because of their physical characteristics (now darting, now stable), metaphysicians have symbolically related them to ideas. Like the fish, ideas dart through the mind, associate with similar ideas (live in schools) and come to rest in the mind only temporarily. Further, in Biblical times most streams and lakes teemed with an abundance of fish, just as the mind teems with ideas.

There is an abundance of ideas also in the great sea of Cosmic Consciousness. Perhaps it was in connection with this that Jesus was motivating the disciples when he told them to launch out into the deep and let your nets down for a draught. Or when he told Peter he would find tribute money in the first fish he would thereafter catch.

After the Resurrection he stood on the shore, at first unrecognized, and when the disciples told him they had caught nothing throughout the previous night and had nothing to eat, he told them to cast the net off the *right* side of the ship. They drew in 153 fish.

A numerologist would tell you that 153 reduces to nine, the number which signifies completion and preparation for a new beginning — the number of the person who has achieved an initiation and is ready to begin a new and higher cycle.

If you can conceive of the physical body as the boat temporarily used by the incarnated mind, and if you remember we previously discussed the right side of the brain as the terminal through which spiritual and creative ideas flow, then in the allegory just given you can understand why the disciples were told to cast their nets on the right side of the boat. "Turn to the spiritual and creative aspect of your Self for the greater sustenance that will enhance your life."

Astrologically, the age of Pisces (the fish) was just beginning at the time of Jesus. Perhaps the symbol which designated the Piscean Age came into common use due to the astrological inclinations of the early Christians, Essenes and other mystically oriented groups.

It is an age of transmutation (as is every age in its own way) from physical to spiritual, specifically centered in the range from emotional to mental. Fish, along with bread, was the food that was multiplied so the multitude might be fed. Is this not saying that ideas multiply in the mind when treated with the spiritual disciplines and thus satisfy the spiritual hunger of those who aspire?

One gets the feeling of calm assurance in the story of Jesus feeding the multitude. And it tells me that if I engage in spiritually oriented meditative disciplines this will awaken a flow of ideas . . . sufficient to satisfy the needs of any given endeavor; whether material or spiritual.

Throughout· the Bible, the swine is another important animal. In most instances the swine is despised as a repository of accumulated impurities, whether in the food they are fed or in the ideas they symbolize.

There is a legend that before the swine degenerated in human esteem it had been revered as the animal which taught humankind how to plow. Watching the swine root for food, man learned to plow and sow. Man rewarded his teacher with food, but in time lost sight of the origin of his lesson and discovered that the swine would eat what he refused.

In time, therefore, the swine was considered unclean, and taboo in some cultures, and thus became the appropriate animal to serve as the villain in the story of the prodigal son. After demanding his *material* inheritance, the son left his father's house to become totally immersed in the material world. He squandered his inheritance and became the bond servant of one who owned a herd of swine. He was so destitute that as he fed the swine he hungered for their food. Suddenly an awakening dawned in his consciousness, and he returned to his father's house where he was welcomed with a feast.

The story of the prodigal son is a common story of incarnation . . . the descent of spirit into matter followed by its ascent into spiritual realms again. It is also the story of the transmutation of the consciousness from one orientation to another.

From the Father's House we demand a material inheritance by our exclusive focus on worldly life and possessions. In effect, we become bond servants of the swine owner. Next we realize that such a lifestyle doesn't bring us the kind of happiness we seek, the kind we once knew and of which we have an inner remembrance. There is an awakening to the true source of accomplishment . . . and we return to the Father's House, symbolically the place of spiritual understanding in the consciousness.

"Wilt thou lay down thy life for my sake? Verily, verily, I say unto thee, the cock shall not crow till thou hast denied me thrice." That was the prophecy.

In a very few hours it was fulfilled. "Peter then denied again: and immediately the cock crew."

This incident too has its hidden symbology. The cock crows at the time when darkness is ending but the light has not yet fully arrived. So it was with Peter's denial, both literally and figuratively. His mind had nearly done with the darkness of old concepts and personal characteristics but the new hadn't quite fully dawned in his consciousness.

Quite probably this Biblical incident gave rise to the once held superstition that the cock crows to warn evil spirits it is time for them to cease their ugly affairs, for the light is coming. At the same time the cock's crowing let human inhabitants know they could now leave their homes safely without fear of molestation by those whose activities were conducted in the dark. The cock, therefore, became revered as the herald of the dawn and the animal which helped rid the countryside of evil spirits, robbers, and marauding animals—no small feat indeed.

". . . be ye therefore wise as serpents . . . ." Reptiles are mysterious animals. Their movements are soundless and without visible means of locomotion. They do not visibly age. In the annual shedding of skin they seem to have discovered the secret of eternal youth. In their natural habitat their habits are hardly known to human beings. At a time when the ability to kill one's enemy was a mark of distinction, the serpent gained a reputation for doing so with a minimum of effort, a tiny bite being sufficient to cause a truly mysterious death. For all these reasons they were considered wise.

During the Exodus, Moses and his followers were stung by swarms of "fiery serpents," resulting in illness and death frequently enough for him to discuss the problem with God. He was told to make a serpent of brass and mount it on a pole. Any person who was stung was to look upon the brazen serpent which would serve as an antidote to the poison.

In the Gospel of Mark, the arisen Jesus is reported to have said, "In my name . . . they shall take up serpents . . . and it shall not hurt them . . . " There are cults in the hill country of Kentucky and Tennessee which take this passage literally and include the handling of poisonous snakes as part of their religious worship.

One interpretation of the passage is that Jesus wasn't literally referring to serpents but to one's human enemies which he likened to serpents. If you achieve a spiritual state of consciousness your enemies cannot harm you . . . you are always superior to them.

The serpent grasping it's own tail with it's mouth was an ancient symbol of immortality. The upraised serpent, as in the cobra headdress of the ancient Egyptian kings, was a symbol of wisdom and superiority. The fact that Jesus would use the phrase "wise as serpents" would certainly indicate the probability that he was familiar with Egyptian and Hindu Mystery School techniques. In India there once existed the Order of the Nagas whose insignia was the serpent on the head, indicating the attainment of wisdom through arousing the kundalini, the sleeping serpent within that, when properly aroused, becomes the fiery serpent of illumination.

The serpent in the Garden of Eden represents the opposite polarity of wisdom. In the Hindu tradition it would be the kundalini fire directed toward lustful sex rather than spiritual illumination.

So the serpent symbol had its dual meaning, just as the human being has a dual nature, one aspect directed toward the physical and impermanent, the other toward the spiritual and eternal.

VEGETATION

Sometime, somewhere, an ancient philosopher and naturalist must have speculated upon the Divine Life while wandering through a forest.

"Plants and shrubs and trees grow and multiply in mysterious ways not visible to humankind," he would say to himself. "It is obvious that the divine life surges through *them* as well as us. Therefore, it is sacred.

"Vegetation lives on and on in spite of fire and flood and the hand of man," he would reason. "Therefore, it is obviously immortal."

Then a compelling thought would strike his consciousness. A true inspiration. "If the divine life is present in these plants and shrubs and trees, and if they withstand adverse elements, whether natural or human, then they must be able to heal human wounds and ills."

Thus was born one of the medical sciences.

And our long ago friend might have mused further. "If the divine life is so wonderfully present in these objects perhaps they provide ways to help the human kingdom reach the Divine. Possibly they could serve either as inspirational symbols or as direct stimulants to the consciousness."

Thus was born one of the spiritual sciences.

And in mystical science there is the concept that every kind of vegetation is sacred . . . immortal . . . healing. The fact that we do not know the healing virtues of a certain plant doesn't mean they do not exist; we simply have not yet discovered them.

"And God said, Behold, I have given you every herb bearing seed, which is upon the face of all the earth, and every tree, in the which is the fruit of a tree yielding seed; to you it shall be for meat."

Modern research has confirmed the health giving properties of hundreds of plants, and there are many who accept the ancient idea that for every illness in the human kingdom there is a natural antidote in the vegetable kingdom. But our principal interest is in the mystical significance which various forms of vegetation have for us. Let us examine the largest first.

Trees. No object in nature better illustrates Hermes' dictum, "As above, so below." As the branches and leaves draw sustenance from the upper atmosphere so the roots draw life from the earth. In a similar fashion humankind draws on a Higher Life for sustenance while absorbing food from the earth to maintain physical life.

The two most famous of all symbolical trees were in the Garden of Eden: the Tree of Life, and the Tree of the Knowledge of Good and Evil.

There was no prohibition against eating the fruit of the Tree of Life. To the esotericist it is symbolic of the sympathetic nervous system by which life forces in the human body are more or less automatically regulated.

The Tree of the Knowledge of Good and Evil is representative of the cerebro-spinal nervous system. Its energies should be transmuted to wisdom. However, when its energies are misdirected to satisfy only the physical to the exclusion of mental and spiritual appetites, then the human being is vibrationally separated to a greater than ever degree from the source of Wisdom, and problems therefore arise.

The symbolism of a tree is frequently extracted from the nature of the tree. The evergreen, with its year 'round foliage, symbolizes eternal life. The olive, a source of food, treasured cooking oil and fuel for lamps, also prized because it relieves pain, is the symbol of peace. The first oil from the pressed olive was considered the purest and therefore dedicated to temple use. The almond, a high protein nut of tremendous life giving quality, is a symbol of authority. Aaron's almond rod budded overnight when placed in the temple with the rods of other persons, thus insuring his selection as priest.

Abraham pitched his camp by the Oaks of Mamre, and their sturdiness and stability were transmuted to him and his followers. The fig and its sweet fruit, maintaining its flavor even though dried, represents the joy of the life to come. It is believed that the ointment applied to the wounded wayfarer by the Good Samaritan was a combination of fig and olive. The mistletoe was revered because of its healing properties and its year 'round hardiness.

Jesus was crucified upon a tree in the form of a cross, which emphasizes another form of symbology: the tree as a sacrifice of the physical to higher wisdom. Incense derives from the resins of vegetation. The temple fires were built only of carefully selected woods, which were blessed in dedicatory ceremonies by the priesthood.

Palms and dates provided healing ointments, related by the disciples to the healing ministry of Jesus and thus their use in church ritual.

In addition to the symbolic aspects already mentioned, there is the seven candled candelabrum, a symbol derived from the burning bush which was not consumed and from which God spoke to Moses.

So the tree has been unique in the services it has provided humankind: food, fire, light, healing ointment, clothing, shelter, and inspirational symbolism.

"I am the vine and you are the branches" was the phrase Jesus used to symbolize the idea that he is in you and you are in him and we are all part of the same life.

The fruit of the vine was a factor in Jesus' first miracle at the marriage feast in Cana when he turned water into wine. How did he actually accomplish this feat? Did he implant the vibratory essence of a higher life into the lower, did he accelerate a lower vibratory substance until it merged with a higher? From either viewpoint, transmuting water into wine is symbolic of transmuting the consciousness to a higher level of expression. The first miracle is also symbolic of the last, transmuting the physical body into a body of spirit or a higher vibratory nature.

Wine appeared again at the Lord's Supper. "I will not drink henceforth, of this fruit of the vine until that day when I drink it new with you in my Father's kingdom," he said, referring again to the higher level of consciousness which the wine symbolically represented.

Wheat possesses two symbolic meanings, different but related: eternal life and fertility. Jesus deftly incorporated both in a single statement at the time it became obvious his final hours on earth were near. "Except a corn (kernel) of wheat fall into the ground and die, it abideth alone. But if it die, it bringeth forth much fruit."

In a more mystical sense, he was saying that when the consciousness dies to the lower physical senses, it becomes alive to the higher spiritual senses.

The mustard seed is about half the size of the head of a pin. The tree which springs from it is one of the largest. That is why Jesus used the mustard seed as a symbol of faith. The catalytic and ever expanding action of a grain of faith often causes the removal of mountains (obstacles, perverse circumstances, etc.).

If the faith which is concentrated in your consciousness is equivalent to the life force compacted in the mustard seed, and if you sow it in the proper places and under the proper conditions, ". . . nothing shall be impossible unto you."

Another symbol arising from vegetation is the crown of thorns. "And when they had pleated a crown of thorns, they put it on his head."

In Biblical times, it was customary to place a crown of thorns upon the heads of the worst criminals prior to death by crucifixion. Legend says that the one placed on the head of Jesus became a halo.

Some esotericists attach a mystical symbolism to the practice. They feel that the cranial nerve endings, possibly the most sensitive in the body, are especially significant to the Third Eye area. Just as the cross symbolizes the sacrifice of the physical self to free the spiritual, so the crown of thorns represents sacrificing the physical sensitivities in order to activate the higher psychic receptors, symbolized by the traditional halo—also circular in shape but placed above the physical head rather than in contact with it.

PLACES

The earth itself, of course, is a receptacle filled with all manner of vibratory energies. "Put off thy shoes from off thy feet for the place whereon thou standest is Holy ground," were the words that came to Moses from out of the burning bush. Apparently, at that particular location a concentration of vibratory energies made the phenomena possible. The admonition to remove his shoes focused Moses' concentration upon his role in the situation—telling him that he was to be psychically receptive to the occurrence.

AMULETS—CHARMS

Other receptacles of life force—non-living in the normally accepted sense of life—are inanimate objects such as amulets and charms. They were banned by the early Church to avoid the promotion of object worship in place of personality adoration.

However the personality seemed to depart, whether by the separation of physical distance or through death, the amulet and charm remained physically available. Therefore, they served either as a temporary stand-in or permanent substitute for those who required something tangible on which to focus their spiritual feelings and aspirations.

Amulets and charms, of course, have always existed since humankind searched for some material way to express non-material feelings. Perhaps there is some basis in fact for their use. Those who understand the atom tell us that every solid object consists of atoms. They, in turn, are composed of particles and sub-particles in constant motion. We are also told that the human consciousness acts upon the particles and sub-particles in ways that science does not as yet fully comprehend. Thus, each object has its degree and level of animation, conditioned by any person who uses it.

If the mind in a projective mode affects a solid object, then it may be very reasonable to assume that the mind in a receptive mode is responsive to that object. The vibratory condition carried by an amulet or a charm may thus be built up by its owner, then discharged back to him when he becomes attuned to it for the purpose of receiving its blessing, or "good luck" as some would have it.

The ephod or priest's breastplate described in the 28th chapter of Exodus, used for divination, is an example of a highly sophisticated charm which had official sanction for its use. Precious stones were used in making it, and gems thus became deeply revered as charms. The vision of the heavens described in the 21st chapter of Revelations included precious stones, adding at a different time further impetus to the use of gems in amulets and charms.

Animal and human relics have also long served as articles of good fortune or as centers for the focus of religious awe and inspiration. Bones, hair, and articles of clothing became spiritual treasures to the believer and financial treasures to the unscrupulous.

The possessions of one's ancestors, pictures, medals, anything touched by a holy person—all these and countless other items have served as focal points of contact with individuals, energy levels, wished-for good fortune, healing, and many other purposes.

The apostle Paul blessed pieces of cloth (described in various translations as handkerchiefs, garments, scarves) for persons who were ill. The theory is that by blessing the cloths he imparted a vibrant healing quality to them. By placing the cloths on the bodies of those who were ill, the energy was released to them and they were made whole.

THE CROSS

Purveyors who preyed upon human gullibility found a ready market for the cross as a relic which they could peddle at great profit. Someone once estimated that if all the fragments of the cross on which Jesus was purported to have been crucified, could be assembled in a single block of wood, it would require three hundred men to lift it! It was explained by the hawkers that the cross had the unusual property of proliferating itself because the blood of Jesus gave it a peculiar kind of life force. In this manner, there came into being endless fragments of that historic crucifixion device.

The cross as a symbol of the crucifixion has become the amulet of Christianity. In earlier times, when used in ritual, it was usually painted either green to signify that it was from a tree or red to symbolize the blood of Jesus.

Christian symbolism includes two kinds of crosses which have become, in effect, the official amulet. The first is the "Cross of Passion." It was usually painted green to signify that it was from a tree. The second is the "Cross of the Resurrection." This might be said to be the spiritual counterpart of the Cross of Passion. It was painted either blue, signifying the heavens, or white, the color of Divinity.

OIL

Oils, ointments, perfumes—essences extracted from flowers, fruit, berries, and many types of vegetation—are often treasured for their purity and scarcity. Because of those two qualities they have become precious and thus through all time have served as revered charms.

The immoral woman who anointed Jesus' feet with oil from her alabaster flask was accorded a higher place in his esteem than the Pharisee whose knowledge and wealth were far superior to hers. The epistle of James counsels that anyone who is ill should be prayed for and anointed with oil by the leaders of the church.

The very first oil of a crop was treasured for ceremonial purposes. It contained fewer impurities than later pressings and was therefore symbolic of a higher purity than normally expressed. It was also more expensive which symbolized the value of spiritual wisdom.

*   *   *   *   *

Mysticism is a process of discovering and expressing the relationship between differentiated life and the Universal Life.

*   *   *   *   *

SELF-DISCOVERY GUIDE IV

What are your likes and dislikes in relation to the world around you?

To analyze your affinities is to make real discoveries about your own nature. To feel comfortable with certain aspects of the world around you is to discover inner harmonies with the outer world that lead to stability of mind and emotions and thus even to improved physical condition.

Make a list of items discussed on the preceding pages. Use pencil to mark your preferences in the order of your choice. Place on the first line the object or the item with which you feel most comfortable. Use pencil because you may wish to indicate different choices after you have completed your list, or at some later time.

The question to ask yourself is, "With what kind of other than human life do I have the greatest affinity?"

ANIMALS	VEGETABLES	PLACES	SIMPLE OBJECTS

Upon learning in this organized way that there are forms of non-human life with which you have great affinity, and by including them more prominently in your life, you create the outer environment which stimulates the inner life. To be comfortable in your relationship with your surroundings (and I'm not speaking of luxurious "creature comfort") is to induce a favorable atmosphere for personal spiritual awareness.

CHAPTER 5

THE MANY PATHS TO GOD

The ways of the mystics are many and varied. Each of them somehow finds a Path which leads to the Goal.

The Path may be discovered over the years through slow, sometimes painful, personal experience and study. Or it may reveal itself with the electric suddenness of a burning bush from which the "very voice of God" speaks in transforming tones.

The true mystic speaks or writes of his own experiences with a certain futility, knowing well that the close and intimate detailed intricacies, as well as the expansive and vast vistas can be truly appreciated only by the individual beholder. Yet there's a compulsion to try in order that others might find an equally inspiring way. It isn't a desire to feel superior. It's an overwhelming wish to share.

It's really difficult to discuss the many great mystics and their uniquely individual Paths. In this chapter, I'll try to present a representative group of them, condense their individual methods to as few words as possible, and indicate the starting points of their several Paths which you may then wish to explore further in the process of finding your own way.

Remember that it is almost impossible to transmute an experience into a doctrine. God is a spiritual experience (and that just might be as good a definition of God as any) and cannot be contained or confined in a man-made doctrine, inspiring though it may be.

There was a time when it was believed that persons having mystical experiences were pathological—while those who simply accepted mystical ideas were merely weird. That was the difference between phenomena and doctrine. Neither were socially acceptable.

"I've had a vision," says the mystic.

"You've had a hallucination," says the non-mystic.

Is there a way to know whether or not a personal experience is one or the other of these? Vision or hallucination? Genuine or counterfeit? Valid or false?

St. Teresa of Avila, a Spanish Carmelite nun, is accepted as one of the great mystics. She experienced visions. She believed herself "caught up" into the heavens. Many thought she was having hallucinations. Others were convinced she was ensnared by Satan. How did she respond to their disbelief and criticism?

She affirmed that you can only judge by the change which occurs in a person who has had a true mystical experience. She also pointed out that those who do not have such experiences are usually uncomfortable in the presence of those who do. For instance, a contemporary of St. Teresa's was jailed by his fellow Carmelite monks because of his "visions." Thus a religious community jailed one of its own members for having a religious experience!

Before her own religious experience occurred, St. Teresa apparently had possessed a very unpleasant personality. She was transmuted by the experience into an angelic being, a person of tremendous joy from whom emanated the essence of harmony and upliftment.

One test of the mystical experience, then, is its result. "By their fruit," it has been said, "shall ye know them." Let us look at a few representative classical mystics as a way of learning nine mystic paths and the methods of following them. The nine paths which these mystics exemplify include unity through struggle, negation, anticipation, waiting, trial, yielding, psychism, understanding self and spiritual action.

I shall speak for these Great Ones as though they were actually in conversation with you. I do not mean to be presumptuous. It is merely my method of conveying the gist of their ideas.

UNITY THROUGH STRUGGLE

¶ SAINT AUGUSTINE, 354-430 A.D. St. Augustine was a Manichaean, an adherent of a religious philosophy which combined Christian and Persian ideas. He believed there was an eternal struggle between the powers of light and darkness. These powers were conceived of as battling in the world on every level—between nations, between communities, between individuals, and within individuals. It was even considered that the battle continued in the next world.

Through a series of philosophical changes in his own consciousness, St. Augustine experienced a spiritual crisis and was converted to Christianity. He rose to high position and finally became Bishop of Hippo in North Africa. If he were speaking to you now he would say something like the following:

"Your soul possesses an eye capable of most unusual sight. It has the power to behold the Light Unchangeable. Unlike the light of the sun which changes constantly in color, intensity and direction, the Light Unchangeable is the same in every respect forevermore.

"Through the Light Unchangeable there comes a voice from on high. It will say to you as it has to me, 'I am the food of grown men; grow and thou shalt feed upon Me; nor shalt thou convert Me, like the food of thy flesh, into thee, but thou shalt be converted into Me . . . .'

"When you take the Light Unchangeable into your being, the Light does not become what you are. You become what It is."

Thus the eternal struggle between the lesser light and the Greater Light is constant, and it is up to you to absorb as much of the Greater as you possibly can in order to gain victory over the lesser. How is it to be done?

¶ SAINT AUGUSTINE'S METHOD. "Meditate. Turn to your inner self and let your consciousness enter it. Become aware of the Light Unchangeable. It is always there. It is truly part of your eternal being. You share much with It.

"If you will comprehend It sufficiently, you will be elevated by It. You will experience Its ecstasy. Your nature will be converted into Its nature. You will have overcome the world."

UNITY THROUGH NEGATION

¶ DIONYSIUS. The true identity of this mystic isn't known. He may have been a Syrian monk who lived somewhere between 500 and 700 A.D.

Because many of his writings were "anti-organization" he preferred not to take credit for them himself, probably in fear of his life. He ascribed them, therefore, to Dionysius the Areopagite, a person briefly described in the 17th Chap-

ter of Acts as being a follower of Paul. Unity through negation isn't easy to understand or follow.

"Beyond the light visible to your eyes there is a Greater
Light. Beyond *that* Light lies the Divine Darkness. Beyond
the Divine Darkness is God.

"What may become visible to you in a mystical experience is merely a symbol of the Divine Darkness, or that
which is immediately below God. Therefore you do not
really come in touch with God but with the undifferentiated
emanations of God.

"Do not try to make God human by conceiving of him
as having human attributes. God transcends *all* attributes.
Reflections of His qualities pass through the Divine Darkness into the Light and from there into your consciousness."

¶ DIONYSIUS' METHOD. "Follow the via negativa, the
negative way, by purification of the self as the first step. Shed
from yourself every impure quality or attribute. When
Moses first descended from the Mount it was a descent into
impurity and the tablets of the law were broken. After
purification Moses successfully brought them to the people.

"As the second step you must separate yourself from the
outer impurities you encounter in life. Persons, situations,
communities, which are impure must be cast from your life.
Unceasing renunciation of self is required.

"A statue is carved by chipping off every portion of stone
which makes no contribution to its form and beauty. Ab-
stract from your life all that hinders your vision of the
Light."

A certain form of Hindu meditation follows a similar
"negative way" pattern. In it you meditate and when in
touch with your inner self you begin a critical self-appraisal
by describing what you are not. "I am not the body", you

might say. "I am not the senses. I am not the mind." You continue these statements of negation as far as you can. Ultimately, by stating what you are not, through a sudden, dramatic change in your consciousness you come to realize what you really are. It isn't actually a new realization, however. It's simply arriving at that point in consciousness at which you can *recall* what you are in your real essence.

UNITY THROUGH ANTICIPATION

¶ MEISTER JOHANNES ECKHART. Meister Eckhart was a Dominican monk. The date of his birth is not known but the year 1260 is often given. Most writers compare his philosophy with that of the Hindu mystic Sankara. At one time he was tried for heresy.

"Beyond God there lies the Godhead, an abiding place of undeveloped potential. The Godhead is unknown and not to be worshiped. It is a place of darkness and formlessness.

"God emanates from the Godhead. Christ emanates from God and is eternally coming to birth in each human soul. In this way the soul becomes the meeting place between God and man."

¶ ECKHART'S METHOD. "Enter the soul-self through the silent times of meditation. As you near the core of your being you begin to experience its glory. You become aware of the birth of the Christ Spirit.

"Through your association with the Christ Spirit you learn and become familiar with its Divine Nature. When you become familiar with any aspect of the Divine Nature you find God."

UNITY THROUGH WAITING

¶ JAN VAN RUYSBROECK, 1293-1381. When he was fifty years old, Ruysbroeck retired as a parish priest and took up residence in an Augustinian monastery. There he lived a life of nearly total contemplation.

"The moral virtues will help you find union with God. Purity of self is required to blend with the Spirit which embodies all purity. Love all beings and all things, without possessiveness of any kind.

"Engage in meaningful acts of worship. Discover for yourself the beauty and meaning of litergy and personal prayer. Let your life be active, yes, but let it also be contemplative for therein will you find your joy and self-identification with the Spirit of God. Balance is essential."

¶ RUYSBROECK'S METHOD. "Gaze within yourself as though looking into a void. Put from your mind the details of your active life. Create a self-emptiness.

"Crave long and ardently for union with God. Can any gold be more desirable? Or fruitful? Lose yourself in Way-lessness—the waiting for a goal without struggling for it. As lovers silently lose themselves in each other, so lose yourself in the undefined rapture which enfolds God and you."

UNITY THROUGH TRIAL

¶ THOMAS À KEMPIS, 1380-1471, probably the author of the famed work, *The Imitation of Christ*, spent 70 years in monastery life. He believed that what you learn about Christianity must be tested in the trials of everyday life where it will be found sufficient to reveal the reality of the eternal life.

"The world in which you live is plagued with trouble and instability. If offers continuing trials, constant change, and no foundation upon which to find peace and security.

"The way to endure it is to immerse yourself in the spiritual life. The way to enjoy it is to fix your attention on Christ. In doing so you will ultimately arrive at that state of mind in which trial and trouble are sweet and spice, giving life that savor which is heaven on earth."

¶ À KEMPIS' METHOD.   "Give spiritual orientation to your inner life. Express selfless love, purely expressed without any personal expectations attached to it. Deny the self totally. Deny the desire for fame. Deny desire for rewards of any kind. Be unconcerned about troubles, enemies, trials of all kinds. After you have conquered yourself, do for others. Then you will live in heaven while yet on earth."

UNITY THROUGH YIELDING

¶ JACOB BOEHME, 1575-1624, was an illiterate German shoemaker. He educated himself. During his boyhood he experienced a psychic vision in which he found a hidden cave and there discovered a huge sum of money. He felt he shouldn't touch the money and left the cave. At that point the vision ended. Later he tried to lead his friends to the cave but could never find it again. He interpreted this to mean that he should be unconcerned about material matters and devoted to the spiritual life. If he spoke to you now he would say something like this:

"Everything exists in the form of opposites: Man and woman, material and spiritual, even good and evil. Opposites are necessary, therefore if you believe in good you must believe in evil. However, you possess the power to emphasize the good and thus negate the evil. You are a microcosm, an exact duplicate of God."

¶ BOEHME'S METHOD. Study: through acquiring knowledge become the best possible instrument of Spirit. Meditate: through becoming quiet coordinate your life with Spirit. Yield: through acquiescence govern your life by the promptings of the Spirit."

UNITY THROUGH PSYCHISM

¶ EMMANUEL SWEDENBORG, 1688-1772, was a scientist and inventor. He is credited with having created plans for the construction of submarines and airplanes. He was also a politician, a member of Sweden's House of Peers and was national assessor of mines. His followers founded the Church of the New Jerusalem.

"Through the proper adjustment of your consciousness you can see with inner vision and hear with an inner ear, as did the Prophets and Disciples. Beings who inhabit the next world, even the very angels of God, may speak to you and become visible to you.

"You can transcend both time and space through the Divine Consciousness that is the kernel of your own consciousness."

Swedenborg's psychic experiences are well known, especially the incident that occurred while he was attending a social gathering 300 miles from Stockholm. Suddenly he "saw" a huge fire covering much of the city. He told the guests of his vision, and dispatches which arrived several days later confirmed that a good portion of the city had indeed burned.

¶ SWEDENBORG'S METHOD. "You possess faculties not expressed in your outer consciousness—intuition, clairvoyance, clairaudience. They constitute your connection with the very highest levels of life, even with God. Develop them, therefore, to live on every level of life and find your unity with the Infinite."

UNITY THROUGH UNDERSTANDING SELF

¶ RALPH WALDO EMERSON, 1803-1882, was a Unitarian minister, then resigned his pastorate but continued to preach, lecture and write. Emerson's *Essays* are filled with mysticism. He fostered what has become known as Transcendental Philosophy which was a combination of Christianity and Hinduism with the addition of what today is called "positive thinking" and metaphysics.

"Your spirit is a highly valued unity in the order and economy of God's creation. In fact, it is a duplicate of the Spirit of God. You are capable of transcending any form in which it might be encased and any limitation which might surround it."

¶ EMERSON'S METHOD. "Be often silent. Silence is a solvent that negates all the limitations of your normal life and frees you to the trascendental life where you can become greater than you seem to be—a universal spirit at one with the Universal Spirit.

"When you are quiet, extraneous ideas will come into your mind. Consider them. Accept or reject them. It is in this process that the real action of life occurs."

UNITY THROUGH SPIRITUAL ACTION

¶ RUFUS JONES, 1863-1948, raised on a farm in Maine, associated with the Society of Friends (also known as the Quakers), was a teacher, lecturer and the author of 57 books. "The one sure way to the Divine Person is through the human person," he said. And here are some other ideas he would give you if he could talk to you now.

"Your life and your religion both are rooted in mystical experience. The mystical process underlies all things. Your part in the process is to establish a meeting between the human spirit and the Divine Spirit and to create ways in which they can communicate and function in mutual and reciprocal correspondence as spirit with Spirit.

"You are a finite-infinite being, not separate from, but one with the Infinite."

¶ JONES' METHOD.   "First, worship with others to aid in building a potent mystical force. 'Where two or three are gathered together in my name, there I am in the midst of them.'

"Second, engage in personal worship through silence and meditation.

"Third, achieve as high as possible a state of spiritual consciousness.

"Finally, act outwardly from the impulse of the inner spiritual activity."

Rufus Jones believed in mysticism not for any purely personal pleasure but for the universal good that resulted from it. As an illustration of his belief in this respect he organized a committee following World War I that gave one meal each day to 1,200,000 starving German children.

Nine great mystics have spoken to you. They have told you of the nine paths to unity: Struggle, Negation, Anticipation, Waiting, Trial, Yielding, Psychism, Understanding Self, Action.

The truth is that each Path includes the other eight. One Path is dominant for each of us, but neither you nor I can totally ignore the others if we are to progress on our journey from the human to the Divine.

*   *   *   *   *

Mysticism is an experiential or doctrinal (or both) expression of the individual Self and its relationship to the Infinite.

*   *   *   *   *

SELF-DISCOVERY GUIDE V

Attempting to duplicate the exact pattern of another person's life is usually not very productive. But to weave creatively certain of their qualities into the fabric of your own design can be inspiringly helpful.

This self-discovery guide, in a very simple way, can help you do just that. All you need do is note brief answers to the questions listed below. Let your own answers spring intuitively from your spiritual center—and let them inspire you to adventures in mystical Self Discovery.

If I were one of the great mystics, what would I *not do* that I am doing now?

1. ....
....
2. ....
....
3. ....
....

What would I *do* that I am not doing now?

1. ....
....
2. ....
....
3. ....
....

*   *   *   *   *

CHAPTER 6

THE MYSTIC AND THE BIBLE

The process of incarnation, the journey from the spiritual dimensions to infiltrate the Self into the physical form being prepared for it, can be very traumatic. Persons who have clinically "died," yet regained life, almost without exception describe their temporary resentment at having to return to the body from the beautiful moments they've been experiencing.

An understanding of mysticism is a way of healing the intellect wounded by incarnation. I know of no greater healer. The mystical life enables you to see through the illusions of life on earth, enables you to endure it, be strengthened by it, and grow from it.

In fact, I believe this is precisely what Jesus, the Master Mystic of all time, was referring to when he said, "Unto you it is given to know the mystery of the kingdom of God, but unto them that are without, all these things are done in parables." (Mark 4:11)

Those who were "without" did not possess the mystical or inner understanding. When that understanding is achieved the mysteries become clear but remain mystical. In the following pages we will explore this by examining a mystical journey of life described in the New Testament, as that journey is related to the outstanding events in the life of Jesus.

105

There are different ways of viewing the Bible. One is that it is a collection of myths. A reason for this view is that many similar stories (occasionally exactly the same) are found in other cultures where they are often presented as legend and folklore and not as "gospel."

Another view is that the Bible is literal history. Obviously much of it is confirmable by historians, archeologists and others who, by their academic disciplines, can verify numerous historical incidents.

Still others believe the Bible to be allegory, stating, "There are hidden meanings in its passages, different in content than the surface appearances."

Finally, there are those who believe the Bible to be a *combination* of myth, history and allegory. In Paul's letter to the Corinthians he said, "We speak the wisdom of God in a mystery, even the hidden wisdom . . ." (1 Corinthians 2:7) He also spoke of being among the ". . . stewards of the mysteries of God." (1 Corinthians 4:1)

Those who become "stewards of the mysteries of God" are the "initiates" who hold a responsibility to use their knowledge wisely and pass it to others in a responsible manner.

Most anyone can point out errors and contradictions in the Bible. However, when it is viewed as a book of mystical experiences, a never ceasing wellspring of spiritual allegory, combined with inspiring history, it begins to quench the aspirant's spiritual thirst on every level of life.

Let us look at the Gospels as "The Story of the Great Journey," the story of incarnation. It's *your* story and, no matter when you were born, it may be beginning right now, for it not only is an incarnational view of your journey, it is also a developmental view. It's the story of your evolvement to a higher state.

I suggest that the major events in the life of Jesus have a mystical, allegorical, symbolic relationship to experiences you encounter in your journey toward becoming a modern mystic. Together, let us look at those events, and see to what extent they reveal your past, present and future.

BIRTH

Theologians become involved in apologies regarding the Immaculate Conception and the Virgin Birth, and not much is settled by their controversies. A number of other cultures also record the birth of avatars to virgin mothers.

Quite probably the Christian doctrine of the Immaculate Conception was instituted because those who believed Jesus to be God couldn't believe that God had a mother who conceived in the normal manner. And the Virgin Birth doctrine is Biblically substantiated by the prophecy quoted in Matthew 1:23 that ". . . a virgin shall be with child, and shall bring forth a son, and they shall call his name Emmanuel, which being interpreted is, God with us."

Motherhood without intercourse is not unknown to science. There is a process known as *parthenogenesis* in certain living species among which such births do occur. Then of course we have today's laboratory conceptions. But the birth story isn't meant to be either theological or scientific. It is mystical.

That which is immaculately conceived in you is a pure thought in your consciousness. That which is virgin born is of the purely spiritual level of your consciousness and without any material level contact whatsoever.

Jesus discussed this very clearly. "Except a man be born again he cannot see the kingdom of God." (John 3:3) To be born again means to arrive at a new level of understanding.

"Except a man be born of water and of the Spirit, he cannot enter into the kingdom of God." (John 3:5) Traditional Christianity interprets this as requiring baptism. Obviously baptism doesn't confer spiritual understanding in either infants or adults. However, water is one of the universal symbols of mind—and when mind is blended with Spirit (". . . born of water and of the Spirit . . .") then the kingdom of God may be entered.

The first step of your journey, then, is spiritual birth. It is quickly followed by the escape to Egypt, the second step.

THE ESCAPE TO EGYPT

In metaphysical symbology, many consider Egypt to represent a place of darkness. However, we must remember that three of the greatest figures of the Bible received education there—Joseph, Moses and Jesus.

Obviously, then, Egypt was a land of superior intellectual stature. It was the home of the ancient Mystery Schools and attracted students of high intellectual caliber from the entire literate world. Esoterically the alchemists (from whom modern chemistry is derived) received their name from the words Al Khem, meaning: from the black land—the soil nearest the Nile, highly prized for its qualities.

Mystically, then, you go to Egypt—the black land— by going within your self, to the depths of your own consciousness where the highest and truest qualities of mind can be found.

Another mystical idea is that after the birth of the Christ within you, there are those who would take the newborn child from you as Herod would have done in the Biblical story. Your "friends" might use scorn, ridicule, social ostracism or other means to accomplish this. You escape to Egypt or your inner self so those who would take or destroy your new found treasures cannot steal them from you.

CONFOUNDING THE SCHOLARS

After Jesus and his parents returned from Egypt, when he was twelve, they visited the temple near Jerusalem. On the journey home Mary and Joseph discovered Jesus to be missing; they returned to Jerusalem and after three days found him being questioned by the "doctors" or scholars in the temple.

Mystically, the "doctors of the law" symbolize pure intellect. Intellect often questions the value of spiritual understanding. Intellect is to be desired, of course, but standing alone it is cold, unfeeling, devoid of understanding and tends to become crystallized. It must be modified with other qualities. It must turn to sources of inspiration and understanding. This is symbolically represented by the presence of the evolving Christ (the boy Jesus) to which the scholars turned for answers to their questions. The awakened spirit, then, must modify the knowledge you've acquired.

BAPTISM BY JOHN

Baptism symbolizes purification. It's a rite of cleansing the physical self, emblematic of dedicating the body to the spirit with the resulting inner awakening. Following Jesus' baptism (Matthew 3:11-17) ". . . the Spirit of God descending like a dove . . ." lighted upon him. The dove is the spiritual flow from On High which adds an additional dimension to the inner awakening.

John's baptism was an outer "initiation" with water. Jesus' baptism was "with the Holy Ghost and with fire" and was an interior initiation to still higher levels of spiritual development.

THE TEMPTATION

Following the purification and initiation of baptism, or the arrival of a new level of insight, Jesus was led by the spirit to the wilderness to be tested. (Matthew 4:1-11) There he fasted forty days and forty nights. So is it in the Journey of the Self.

A new understanding, an awakening, comes to you and you are thrilled by it. Suddenly, however, you encounter an obstacle and must test your awakened consciousness to learn whether or not it really is superior. The outer symbol of the obstacle is the wilderness, a state of confusion regarding the relationship of spiritual to material matters.

In the ancient Mystery Schools (and to some degree in modern ones also) the candidate for initiation was made to participate in a drama wherein he was confronted by robbers, ruffians and other evil-doers. In the drama of the

Christian mysteries, the deterrent to the Journey of the Self is portrayed by Satan.

"Turn the stones into bread," said Satan. "Use your spiritual power to provide food for yourself on the physical level. Satisfy the body." The first temptation, you see, was on the purely physical plane of expression. The next was on a higher level, the mental.

In what some might consder a hallucination, but what we accept as an initiatory experience, a vision, Jesus was taken to Jerusalem and placed upon a pinnacle of the temple. "Cast yourself down. Angels are watching over you and they will not allow you to fall to the ground." This represents an invitation to pervert the use of higher mental powers exclusively for personal safety rather than the general good they can accomplish.

Finally, he was taken to the mountain top where Satan again spoke. "See all the kingdoms of the world. They are yours if only you will bow down and worship me." The mountain top represents the highest spiritual level of consciousness. Divert it to purely worldly matters and you may gain the world, but in the process you lose your own soul. Each time you.acquire some new spiritual understanding, you will also discover that it is in some way tested, as this temptation in the wilderness symbolizes.

THE APOSTLES CALLED

Knowingly or unknowingly, every mystic engages in the process illustrated by the act of calling the apostles. (Mark 3:13-15 and Matthew 10:2-4) Obviously in your personal journey you are not going to ask a dozen other persons to assist you. However, you are going to assemble, balance and harmonize qualities of your Self that will contribute most to the successful completion of your journey. If each apostle represents an essential interior faculty, then you *can* call upon them to make the journey with you.

Peter: Faith

Andrew: Strength (of mind)

James (son of Zebedee):   Judgment

John: Love

Philip: Power

Bartholomew: Imagination

Thomas: Understanding

Matthew: Will

James (son of Alphaeus):   Order

Thaddaeus: Discrimination

Simon: Zeal

Judas: Desire

Matthias (selected later by the apostles themselves to replace Judas):   Spiritual Desire

Paul: Spiritual Will

These are *your* apostles, supporters and fellow sojourners upon the mystical Journey of the Self. Call them. You may wish actually to do this during your meditation periods by attempting to arouse within yourself the presence of the qualities listed above. Select one quality at a time. Think of the process as that of calling your apostles. Ask for this special help in any area of your self you feel necessary. Associating a specific quality with a specific apostle is a "personification technique" that adds forcefulness to the inner process.

THE FIRST MIRACLE

Changing water to wine was the first miracle; it is charged with mystical symbolism. (John 2:1-11)

The miracle occurred at a marriage feast, symbolic of the union of masculine and feminine, positive and negative polarizations in the consciousness. It represents a consummation of the Mystical Marriage in which the lower self is wedded to the Higher Self so that a complete transformation occurs.

Jesus requested that water pots be brought. They were of course made of clay, symbolic of the physical body which in essence is a clay receptacle for liquids of all kinds.

They were filled with water, representing mind or consciousness.

The vibratory nature of the water was changed and it became wine, a symbol of the consciousness elevated to a higher state, the Christed Consciousness.

An interesting sidelight on this first miracle derives from the fact that grapes are the source of wine, relating to another of the Nazarene's statements: "I am the vine and ye are the branches thereof."

Modern spiritual healers often concentrate their attention upon tumblers of water to be drunk as an aid in their therapy. Science tells us the mind does indeed affect the sub-atomic structure of liquids. Perhaps Jesus' first miracle, then, was a demonstration of the power of mind, waiting to be fully confirmed by modern day science. It indicates the hidden power of your own consciousness.

CLEANSING THE TEMPLE

One of the most magnificent ideas ever incorporated into the philosophy of religion is contained in a question written by Paul to the Corinthians: "Know ye not that ye are the temple of God and that the Spirit of God dwelleth in you?"

"Make not my Father's house a house of merchandise," said Jesus as he drove out those who would do so. (John 2:13-17) They represented intentions that were not spiritually committed. Purification of the temple of self is a process that can never cease. However spiritual you become, you are still brought into association with aspects of a lower nature. The more spiritual you become, the more attention you must pay to purification.

The "temple" which you are exists on several levels of your being. Obviously, the first of these is the body. The tables and silver of the moneychangers, solid physical substances, which Jesus overturned and scattered, represent purifying the body by cleanliness, exercise, diet, fasting, all of which "overturn and scatter" physical impurities.

The animals which were being sold for sacrifice were also scattered. Metaphysically, animals refer to your thoughts and emotions. They should not be bartered for money or destroyed in a misguided act of sacrifice.

The doves were ordered taken away. The dove is the symbol of Spirit. The dove caged represents the Spirit inhibited. It was the Spirit in the form of a dove that rested upon Jesus at his baptism.

Thus, we see that purification to the best of your ability is an important step upon your Journey, and it is one of which you must continually be aware.

HEALING

Mind and spirit function in a way that is superior to matter, causing a response whenever they are applied to physical substance. A person may be healed at a distance as was the nobleman's son (John 4:46-54), or in the presence of the healer as was the man at the pool of Bethesda. (John 5:2-9)

Chapter nine is devoted entirely to the subject of healing and the many mystical channels available for that activity. The mystic has for thousands of years, known that illness is not of the physical body only, but is of the whole person. The healing of a person or a circumstance, then, must be a combination of activities on every level of being. All levels must be unified and harmonized.

THE DISCOURSE ON DIVINITY

Following the incident at the pool, where an illness of 38 years seemed to dissolve at the words of Jesus, rigid officialdom charged him with doing an improper deed on the Sabbath. Jesus responded with, "My Father worketh hitherto, and I work," causing further opposition because he seemed to be equating himself with God. (John 5: 17-47)

The gist of the discourse on divinity is that there is a human spirit and a Divine Spirit; the two may be joined, function harmoniously and cause miracles to occur. Further, it is the nature of the works which result from the union of spirit with Spirit that determines the degree of Divinity involved.

THE TWELVE ORDAINED

After your twelve apostles have been "called," summoned to activity in your life, have met their preliminary challenges through being involved in the first miracle, in cleansing the temple and in healing activities, and have been made to conform with the higher Divine Spirit, you are ready to ordain them and send them forth into the outer circumstances of your life to "preach," or bring the word (vibrational nature) of Spirit into active expression. How do you do this?

In your next meditation, think of an incident that is troublesome. Turn to the list of apostles, and the qualities they represent, on page 112, and select the one which could best improve the troubling problem. Then, as you meditate, send that apostle, a personification of the selected quality, into the situation to modify or resolve it—just as a healing energy was sent to the nobleman's son.

Thus, your apostles are sent into the world around you. They go forth to "preach the gospel," taking your "good news" into every situation you specifically select.

THE TEMPEST STILLED

One of the lessons a mystic needs to learn is how to calm the storms of both the outer and inner life. Jesus' followers joined him in a ship at sea where he fell asleep. A violent storm arose creating panic among the disciples who wakened him and implored him to save them. (Matthew 8:23-27)

He said to them, "Why are ye fearful, O ye of little faith?" Then he arose and rebuked the winds and the sea; and there was a great calm.

You can deal with the "storms" of life through the power of your own consciousness. You can rebuke a storm by arousing the inner (sleeping) Christ principle and applying it to the turbulent outer circumstance. *Ask* the Christ Spirit to radiate from you into the storm and with faith await the ensuing calm.

THE MULTITUDE FED

Five loaves and two fishes. Can they feed a multitude? A little boy provided the catalyst with his loaves and fishes. They were blessed, creating a spiritual atmosphere, not just around the food but in the minds of the multitude.

The spiritual atmosphere overcame the selfishness in the gathering, and nearly everyone said, "Well, here in my pouch I have a little extra food; I'll just share it with the others." This is but one of the explanations that has been applied to the seeming impossibility of feeding the five thousand. (John 6:5-14) But the more mystical explanation can be much more meaningful.

Briefly, wheat represents the Divine Life incorporated into human life—and bread represents molding that life into objective, physical form and accomplishment. Fish symbolize random, aimless ideas in the sea of consciousness. However, undirected physical life and intellectual ideas by themselves are limited in their scope, regardless of the potentials they possess. They cannot "feed the multitude," or fulfill their potentials, until a higher and unifying quality is added.

When they were blessed, when the Christ Spirit was united with their dormant potency, their potentials were fully released, their qualities of fulfillment were increased a hundredfold, and the multitude was fed.

Can food actually be multiplied? We are told that matter and energy are the same and interchangeable. If mind can influence energy, as we are discovering, is it not at least theoretically conceivable that energy can be stimulated by mind in such a manner as to increase the amount of substance in which that energy is formed? Perhaps this is a possibility which our laboratory researchers should investigate.

WALKS ON WATER

One night the disciples were in a boat tossed by wind and waves. Seeing their trouble, Jesus went toward them, walking on the water. Peter asked Jesus to help him walk on the water also and Jesus did so. But when Peter turned his consciousness from the Christ to the wind and waves, he began to sink. Jesus streached forth his hand and saved him. (Matthew 14:22-33)

Mind, like the sea, is sometimes calm and sometimes turbulent. When mind is fixed on the Christ Consciousness, it rises above the normal consciousness represented by the water. When it is centered upon troubles and problems, loses its faith, is weighted with doubts, then it begins to sink. The Christ Consciousness enables you to be superior to the turbulent seas of life.

THE TRANSFIGURATION

Peter, James and John went to the mount with Jesus and he became transfigured, visibly and audibly "overshadowed" by Moses and Elias who had left physical life hundreds of years prior to this psychic occurrence. A tremendous glow of light shone through Jesus during the experience. (Matthew 17:1-8)

The mount is the place of initiation—the place where Higher Consciousness prevails. Moses represents law or order, and Elias represents spiritual awareness. The symbology of the incident reveals that when orderliness and spiritual awareness are under the influence of the Christ Consciousness, then a great radiance shines in and through your faith, judgment and love, represented by Peter, James and John. Whenever the inner Deity shines through you, the outer radiance is recognizable.

LAZARUS RAISED

Was Lazarus really dead or not? Jesus first said that he was not dead, but sleeping (in a trance, hypnotized?), and later stated that he was dead. (John 11:1-46)

In mystical terms, to die means to die to physical matters or physical consciousness—not to physical life. (Paul said, "I die daily.") Regarding Lazarus, Thomas said, "Let us also go, that we may die with him." He was not asking the group to engage in a common death wish but to participate in the initiatory process of coming forth to a Higher Consciousness. Death to the physical side of life means birth to the spiritual side.

Lazarus' "grave" was a cave with a stone upon it, symbolic of the limiting physical dimension of life. Jesus said, "Lazarus, come forth." In other words, "Come out of the crystallized, stony frame of physical plane consciousness into the unbound free state of spiritual consciousness." Then Jesus' words were, "Loose him and let him go." Let him be raised, or freed, to the higher consciousness he has achieved.

Nearly every Mystery School, from the time of ancient Egypt to this very day, at some point in the candidate's initiation presents a drama in which the candidate is placed in a cave, tomb or grave, or in some way bound, and is then freed by the aid of a higher power. The name Lazarus is mystically interpreted to mean: God has helped.

THE TRIUMPHAL ENTRY

The triumphal entry is a journey within a Journey, signifying the entrance to a higher state of consciousness—the gateway to Supreme Illumination. (John 12:12-19)

There was no attempt to impress the multitudes, for Jesus rode a donkey. The donkey symbolizes humility. It is also well known as an obstinate animal. Riding the donkey is symbolic of overcoming the lower self, something that absolutely must be done if one is to achieve spiritual illumination.

THE LORD'S SUPPER

Jesus went with the apostles to the Upper Room (the Higher Consciousness) for the Initiation Feast which was to harmonize on a higher level all the qualities which each could contribute. (Matthew 26:17-30) Symbolically it represents fixation and solidification of the Christ Spirit in all aspects of being on every level of life, whether physical, emotional, mental or spiritual.

Mystically, Jesus infused powerful spiritual elements into the bread and wine which were passed to the apostles. Because Judas represented materially directed desire (remember he carried the purse for the group), he was not harmonious with those spiritual elements. His expectations of the higher powers were that they would be used for purely material purposes. Even his betrayal of Jesus may have been done in the hope of intervention by higher powers, the misguided expectation of another miracle, but it was his lesson to learn that while spirit and Spirit often do become one in expression they remain of differing vibratory levels.

GETHESMANE

At the Mount of Olives is the garden of Gethsemane. The olive is a symbol of peace (with one's self as well as with others) and the oil of the olive is a tremendous healing agent. Gethsemane is the olive press, that, by crushing the olive, extracts the good oil and the refuse is then discarded. In life it is sometimes an agonizing process. (Matthew 26:30-45)

There is an alchemy of sorrow. No mystic ever lived who did not experience it. Every fabric of life has the thread of sorrow woven somewhere in it. If you truly love, there will be times of misunderstanding, confusion, indifference, possibly even betrayal and separation.

"If it be possible, let this cup pass from me: nevertheless not as I will, but as Thou wilt." He was experiencing the initiation of sorrow. The disciples were asleep and Jesus was experiencing that stark, mystic, temporary moment of aloneness with God. This is one of the initiatory steps we all must take on the path to the Great Initiation.

THE JUDGMENT

In your journey along the mystic pathway, you come to a time when you discover that formalism, intellectualism and man-made law often conflict with the Spirit, judge it and even convict it.

Jesus was subjected to three trials, each presided over by a different judge. (John 18:13-38) The first judge was Annas, representing formalism. The second was Caiaphas, symbolic of intellectualism. And the third was Pilate, emblematic of man-made law, who delivered Jesus to the mob.

Remember that you must be subject to man's law, giving to Caesar what is Caesar's, nevertheless the Spirit is separate from it and in your inner consciousness cannot be subordinate to it.

THE CRUCIFIXION

Golgotha, the place of the skull, was the scene of the Crucifixion. As in other initiatory dramas, the skull is also a cave. It is the physical level repository guarding the psychic Third Eye. It houses both intellect and the higher consciousness—and is the place where the intellect is "destroyed" in order that the Spirit might triumph. (Luke 23:24-46)

The cross is not unlike the physician's caduceus. The physician relieves you of physical pain. The cross (of liberation) relieves you of physical form entirely that you might function totally in spiritual form.

The cross is a universal symbol found in numerous forms and in many cultures. It denotes balance between the masculine and the feminine. The center of the cross also represents the spinal column through which rises the kundalini, or divine fire. The cross also represents a person with arms outstretched, and thus symbolizes physical matter from which we are released into spirit.

There were two other crosses upon which thieves were crucified. The first thief represents the physical dimension which will steal from your spiritual understanding if possible. The second thief represents the emotional dimension which *can* be regenerated. Remember that Jesus said to the second thief, "Today shalt thou be with me in Paradise," meaning that whereas the physical is left behind, the emotional nature is actually taken with you into the spiritual dimension.

The Gospels of Matthew and Mark quote Jesus as lamenting, "My God, why hast thou forsaken me?" As though God would desert Jesus at such a time! Dr. George Lamsa, in his translation from the Aramaic, Jesus' native tongue, has it: "My God, for this was I born." In other words, "This is my destiny."

Each of us is crucified many times. Sometimes by circumstances, sometimes by other persons. We must realize that crucifixions are openings that enable us to rise to a higher level. As Luke quotes Jesus, "Father, into thy hands I commend my spirit."

THE RESURRECTION

Except for the crucifixion there is no resurrection. What really happened to the body of Jesus? If water can be transmuted to wine, is it not conceivable that physical substance can be transmuted to spiritual substance? Science tells us that mind can change the vibratory rate of sub-atomic particles. Supramind, such as the mind of Jesus, acting upon the body in the tomb, could in my opinion sufficiently alter its vibratory rate so that he could pass through seemingly solid substance. (John: 20)

Atoms that had been vivified and spiritualized over a lifetime, as Jesus' surely were, would be specially susceptible to mental influence. So it might not have required too great an effort on his part. Therefore, I'm ready to accept the idea of a literal transmutation of his body, leaving behind an amazingly empty tomb.

But the resurrection is symbolic also. It denotes a transmutation of consciousness, a refinement of its structure, so that never again are physical plane limitations accepted as final.

THE RETURN

Following the resurrection, Jesus returned to be seen and heard on numerous occasions. He talked to the Marys and other disciples, he appeared in the Upper Room, he walked and talked with the men on the way to Emmaus, explaining the Scriptures and restoring new life to the despondent consciousness they were experiencing. Emmaus means: medicinal springs. (John 21 and 22)

Symbolically, the return means that when you achieve any height of spiritual understanding (and there will be a series of such achievements), you return briefly and partially to express your new found level of understanding before going on to still greater heights.

THE ASCENSION

The Ascension is the moment of total freedom from the vibratory magnetism of the physical plane. It may apply to a specific experience while you are yet upon this plane in the physical body and it may apply to that time when, as in the Hindu philosophy, you are freed from the wheel of necessity and need never again incarnate unless you will to do so. It is the time of complete release from and victory over the physical. (Mark 16:19)

*   *   *   *   *

The journey is a long one. As the twenty-four steps of it are given here, they are fairly chronological in the life of Jesus so far as the more mystical and initiatory aspects and experiences of His life are concerned. If you will look at your own life, you are apt to note that they relate to the experiences *you* are having also. In this sense, they are not only symbolic and initiatory, they are universal. You may thus possess the mystical knowledge that on the great Journey of the Self you walk with the Christ.

*   *   *   *   *

Mysticism is a method of healing the trauma
of incarnation.

*   *   *   *   *

SELF-DISCOVERY GUIDE VI

Study the following list of the twenty-four steps in the Journey of the Self. Purely for your own satisfaction and self-understanding, check those which you've experienced, either actually in outer situations or mystically in your consciousness—or in some instances, possibly both.

STEPS TAKEN	ACTUALLY	MYSTICALLY
Birth: attaining a new level of understanding		
Escape to Egypt: journey to the inner self		
Confounding the Scholars: breaking up the crystallized consciousness		
Baptism: awakening through purification and dedication		
Temptation: the new understanding is tested		
Apostles Called: mobilizing and unifying your inner qualities		
First Miracle: using the dormant power of your own consciousness		
Cleansing the Temple: spiritual purification and commitment of your inner faculties		
Healing: unifying and harmonizing inner levels of being		
Discourse on Divinity: joining the human spirit and the Divine Spirit		
The Twelve Ordained: using inner faculties to influence outer circumstances		
The Tempest Stilled: radiating the Christ Spirit into the storms of life		

STEPS TAKEN	ACTUALLY	MYSTICALLY
The Multitude Fed: further incorporating the Divine Life into the physical life		
Walks on Water: calmness and Assurance attained through Christ Consciousness		
The Transfiguration: outer radiance gained through inner orderliness and spiritual awareness		
Lazarus Raised: leaving the crystallized lower consciousness to achieve the unlimited higher consciousness		
The Triumphal Entry: spiritual illumination through overcoming the lower self		
The Lord's Supper: incorporating the spiritual into the physical		
Gethsemane: discovering the alchemy of sorrow		
The Judgment: giving to Caesar, but maintaining the spiritual consciousness		
The Crucifixion: release from exclusive fixation on the physical level		
The Resurrection: refining and transmuting the consciousness to a higher level		
The Return: expressing your new level of understanding in your present day circumstances		
The Ascension: release from dominance by the physical into the freedom of the spiritual		

CHAPTER 7

THE MYSTIC AND THE SCIENTIST

Perhaps a chapter about science shouldn't begin with a legend. But because it provides us with insights about mysticism *and* science I'll tell it anyway.

Once there were two knights who lived during the flower of knighthood in separate areas of a country named Maranga. Separately they set out upon a Quest—which was to perform a worthwhile service for their country. They had sworn to die in its honor if need be.

Shortly after they had gone abroad, the residents of Maranga held a meeting to protest the name of the country, which they did not like. They decided to change it to Pacoma.

Now two other knights in the same land also decided to go upon a Quest for the honor of their country, which of course was now named Pacoma. They, too, swore to give their lives if necessary.

Several months later one knight from each group happened to encounter each other. The first knight drew his sword and shouted, "Long live Maranga." The second knight responded by drawing his weapon and shouting, "Long live Pacoma."

Their battle was terrible indeed. It ended only when both nearly exhausted knights simultaneously lunged at each other and, with true swordsmanship, took each other's life. The other two knights will not meet until later.

The point of the story thus far is that they both died for the same country, the same ideal, the only difference between them being the different terms each used to designate it.

In a sense, that describes the relationship between science and mysticism. To an amazing extent the two are parallel. Yet they've been at odds for centuries. They haven't really learned that only the name of the country has been changed —it is mainly the terminology that starts their swords to flashing.

In this chapter we will investigate some of the surprising similarities between mysticism and science. You must understand, of course, that I am not a scientist, so my view is more mystical than scientific—which in the light of the legend of the two knights may mean nothing at all.

I'll begin by quoting a scientist. About 1925 Charles Steinmetz, one of the scientific greats of our time, said, "Some day the scientists will turn their laboratories over to the study of God and prayer and the spiritual forces which as yet have hardly been scratched." At this point in time and during the years to come we shall be privileged to see— indeed we are seeing—his prophecy come true.

Mysticism and Science have a common ancestry. Both spring from the same source. Superstition and magic in earlier times gave rise to the body of truths with which they superficially dealt. They seemed to follow different paths, but like the two knights they met occasionally and too often the result was a battle. I would say that, in modern times, "Mysticism is science from a religious point of view. Science is mysticism from a non-religious point of view."

The dictionary describes science as a branch of knowledge or study which systematically arranges a body of facts or truths and shows the operation of general laws regarding those facts or truths.

If you will substitute the word mysticism in place of science the same definition holds true. Mysticism also is a branch of knowledge or study which systematically arranges a body of facts or truths and shows the operation of general laws regarding those facts or truths.

One of the differences between the two is that science is organized into *group,* academic and experiential structures —whereas mysticism's structures, though experiential, are usually *individual* and non-academic. Each individual mystic knows he is dealing with a body of facts, that he has them systematically arranged in his own consciousness, and that they show the operation of Cosmic Law, or the laws of God.   Mysticism and science are really two views of the same truth. Just as you and I, for example, would look at the Great Pyramid from the same vantage point yet describe it differently, so do mysticism and science differently describe the same reality. With each passing year their encounters are more frequent and, happily, less antagonistic. There is a dawning realization in the minds of both that they are champions of the same country, and that they are fufilling the Steinmetz prophecy. Let us examine more of that common ground.

WHAT BOTH SEEK

Looking to the basic goals of both the mystical and scientific disciplines, we discover that each has its sight set upon arrival at specific destinations. A brief list of those intentions enables us to see the common path both are following.

¶ REALITY. Remember the definition of mysticism as the art of union with reality. The mystic finds it in the laboratory of the self. In the research laboratory the scientist, too, seeks to discover what is real and what is illusion.

¶ ULTIMATE TRUTH. To discover something that will never be changed—an idea, a formula, an operating law of the universe. Both disciplines look with fond hope upon such a goal. For each it is *the* Quest. Half truths and untruths are slowly cast aside as we are able to replace them with the truths we discover.

¶ PROOF (OR DISPROOF) OF PRIOR FINDINGS. Both communities have accumulated findings which are accepted as fact. They are, and should be, examined over and over again. Sometimes generations pass and suddenly a prior finding is discovered to be incorrect. As humankind changes on all levels of being, higher views of prior knowledge come into play.

¶ FURTHER REVELATION. The saga of humankind is a journey in knowledge from the unknown to the known, and from the known to a further revelation of additional knowledge. Scientist and mystic may seem to receive their revelations from different sources, but the whisperings of those revelations have a common fountainhead as we shall see throughout this chapter.

¶ ACCEPTANCE BY OTHERS. Both mysticism and science may present what either believes is a new theory, or a newly discovered law—then they ask others to test or accept it. Neither seeks to exercise exclusive rights. Both follow the inner compulsion to share. The request that others accept what is offered is usually accompanied by proof—but both science and mysticism have been known to ask acceptance on faith. As Jesus said, ". . . though ye believe not in me, believe the works . . . ." Faith is asked for in both disciplines.

In these shared goals, mysticism has much more in common with science than does conventional religion. In its ponderously organized way, conventional religion almosts panics at the possibility that it does not yet possess all of reality, the full measure of ultimate truth, or that further revelations might be forthcoming.

"Do not roll away the stone of the tomb we have built around ourselves, for we are unable to step forth into the light of greater understanding." If the organized body of conventional religion could speak, these might be its words. Fortunately, however, they are not the words of many enlightened persons who function within that body.

BOTH HAVE A DOCTRINE

There are texts for both communities which state the basic premises upon which their doctrines are formed. Libraries, bookshops, lectures, classes, pronouncements of all kinds offer the doctrines. In general, these constitute statements of the *external* truths accepted in each discipline.

But there are *internal* truths as well. Give a thousand physicists a text on the atomic structure of the peanut and you will receive a thousand different opinions of its value and power, based upon personal and laboratory observations. Hand a peanut to a thousand mystics, and you'll be given the results of a thousand conversations with the life (and possibly even the intelligence!) it contains. George Washington Carver, a combination scientist and mystic, talked to God in his laboratory about the peanut and the result was several hundred commercial products now used around the world.

There are common basics — and there are individual variations—in the way each scientist or mystic practices his discipline. The scientist says that validity is proved by repeatability and the mystic cannot repeat his experience. But if the experience occurred, it had to be in accordance with the law, which may or may not be known. Nothing happens outside the law. It *could* be repeated if precisely the same conditions were created. In the individual, however, there is a high improbability of this ever being done. The scientist does have more control over the repeatability of his experiences (at least in the laboratory) than does the mystic.

THE PRINCIPLES OF UNCERTAINTY
AND COMPLEMENTARITY

An exact interaction between thought and matter is unrepeatable—thus the principle of uncertainty. That thought and matter do interact is demonstrable—thus the principle of complementarity.

Science has long held that it is impossible to separate the experimenter from the experiment. Unpredictable factors in any experiment, or experience, cause results to change from time to time and render repeatability impossible.

We are told that sub-atomic particles are influenced by consciousness—and that must apply to the scientist in his experimental laboratory and the mystic in his experiential one.

Electric fields *may* be independent of the matter upon which they act, and they may be so fully involved with that matter as to be practically inseparable. In any event, consciousness influences those fields and thus changes the nature of the matter, animate or inanimate, upon which they act.

If the electromagnetic pattern surrounding a polliwog is in the shape of a frog, then the physical form of the polliwog is going to change in accordance with it and become a frog—an idea which may have been inherent in the consciousness of the polliwog all along. *Physical form evolves by the action of consiousness upon it through the electronic fields which surround and permeate it.* What the scientist calls the magnetic field, the mystic refers to as the aura, two names for the same country.

METHODOLOGY

Practitioners of the two disciplines begin with an advance acceptance of their basics. Each holds beliefs in his consciousness concerning laws already accepted, or concerning the main body of understanding among colleagues. If one begins without any preconceived ideas, he has no starting place. So, to both, in the beginning the "bible" is what is already known and generally accepted.

The second step in methodology is that either you agree or disagree with previous findings. You have your own interpretation of those findings, and you determine that either you are going to substantiate or refute them.

Then you take the third step, laboratory experimentation, either scientific or mystic, in an attempt to achieve the result already selected. Harold Higbe, for many years professor of electrical engineering at the University of Michigan, whom I once met by "chance," gave me an encouraging lesson in this step. "I conduct experiments to gain a desired result," he said. "If I'm not successful a thousand times I haven't yet failed. The next time may provide the success I seek." Dr. Higbe was, in fact, talking to me about mystical methodology at a time when I was discouraged with it, and his words were a turning point in my life.

Step four is confirmation. Can it be repeated? Can it be done by someone else? Science wants an exact duplicate of results for confirmation of an experiment or theory. Mysticism must be satisfied with an approximation of repeatability, due to the impossibility of creating precisely the same circumstances in any two given instances.

PSYCHOLOGY AND PSYCHIATRY

There are parallels between the development of the two branches of therapeutic art, psychology and psychiatry, and the development of mysticism.

For example, to the orthodox religionist, the mystic is a heretic. Through the centuries numerous mystics were ostracized, harassed, banished, tortured, even condemned to death. In the earlier days of their professions, the psychologist and psychiatrist met the same opposition and sometimes the same fate, and in some instances still do today. They've had to struggle for acceptance in the medical community. Parapsychology (which, incidentally, one might liken to mystical psychology with a special attempt to avoid religious connotations) has been having its problems in this respect since the 1930's and there are still more to come.

Groups have a history of accomplishing benefits for their members, then moving toward the atmosphere of controlling their members, then to the goal of making the membership exclusive, and finally, with the acquisition of power, of crystallizing on the organization rather than the benefits it can provide. These stages of development aren't well defined and merge into each other. Psychiatry and psychology, and various groups interested in mysticism, share these steps.

The "group spirit" that is generated by these stages often accomplishes a great deal of good. "Where two or more are gathered together in my name, there am I (the Christ Spirit) in the midst of them," can also be applied to the objectives of an organized group.

COMMON CHARACTERISTICS: SCIENTIST AND MYSTIC

All scientists and mystics who have gone beyond a stodgy repetition of the historical state of their respective fields are imaginative and creative individuals. They are also very intuitive.

The scientist might deny his possession of the intuitive faculty. "I simply assemble facts, then rearrange them in a creative manner," he might say. But many scientists do admit the existence of intuition.

Intuition is no substitute for thought. It supplements it. It grasps the significance of the facts in a different way than does the normal consciousness. It provides insights when facts are limited. Superior scientists and mystics, indeed the superior practitioners in any field, find that intuition and thought complement and reinforce each other. Development of intuition causes the mind to become more alert. A keen mind increases intuitive perception.

On a fairly regular basis, modern science is discovering

that mental powers ascribed to mystics are valid, and in many instances can be acquired by "non-mystics" as well. Telekinesis, or the moving of an object by mind power, healing of the self and others, holistic medicine, various states of consciousness, right and left brain functions, biofeedback techniques, body consciousness as well as mind consciousness, ESP, Kirlian photography, control over circumstances and other inner activities are now the province of scientist as well as mystic. Further, science corroborates many of religion's "miracles," changing water to wine for example.

The only unfortunate aspect of this scientific excursion into the once "unknown" which was mysticism, is that science may attempt to appropriate it all as its own province— and thereby extract its spirituality, leaving only the materialistic shell. It is a danger which may be an even greater peril to humankind than the possibility of a nuclear holocaust.

Use Kirlian photography to photograph a dime and a certain energy field is revealed. Concentrate your attention intensely on the dime and a different energy field results. Think a different type of thought—altruistic, materialistic or spiritual, for example, or express different emotions, sorrow, joy, anger, love—and still different energy fields appear.

The scientist has his energy field, and the mystic has his. The mystic often describes his as auras, thought forms, mental and spiritual projections. The scientist describes his as electromagnetic patterns, sine waves and so on. This is an exciting time for humankind, a time when science and mysticism are enriching each other, exploring each other's countries and discovering they are indeed the same.

To complete the legend which opened this chapter, the other two knights finally met. Instead of drawing their swords and dueling for the honor of their country, they engaged in friendly, cooperative conversation. They discovered they were from different parts of the same land, and were merely describing it with a different word. They "joined forces," and walked together in peace and productiveness on the One Path.

* * * * *

Mysticism is the process of enlarging your consciousness from a point to a circle.

* * * * *

SELF-DISCOVERY GUIDE VII

After you've experimented and familiarized yourself with this Self-Discovery Guide until you can practice it without thinking, forget it! When it becomes a habitual act it fosters intuition, imagination, creativity and vital thinking. When you consciously think about it, however, it destroys all four of those paramount inner functions, just as the pianist destroys artistic expression if he thinks about placing each finger on the proper key.

What you wish to do, then, is: 1) Learn the principles, 2) Experiment, 3) Practice, and 4) Express habitually in any given situation.

EXPERIMENT 1

When you think, you create an electromagnetic pattern in and around yourself. It varies with each passing second. It's a reflection of your emotions, thoughts, aspirations, intentions and desires at that exact moment.

At the conclusion of the paragraph you're now reading, put the book down. Sit quietly, breathe a little deeper than usual, release tensions on every level of your being. Then for a time simply realize that you are creating an electromagnetic pattern which reflects your "state of being" at the moment. "Feel it"—not by some physical sense of feeling, but by inner awareness feeling. After you have experimented a few moments, go to Experiment 2.

EXPERIMENT 2

The electromagnetic state is always one of either receiving or transmitting. The pattern of the field is receptive or projective. As flower petals open to receive the rays of the sun, so the electromagnetic state of your being may, at your discretion, be opened to receive vibratory impulses from various possible sources which you also predetermine by the nature of your thought.

Now, after the following instructions, put the book down again. Sit quietly as before. Regulate your breath and release tensions. Consciously direct the nature of your electromagnetic pattern to be receptive. To what? To your own High Self, to other persons either incarnate or discarnate, to Cosmic Consciousness, to God, to the "eternity domain," to a quality such as love. After you "get the feeling" of this state, go to Experiment 3.

EXPERIMENT 3

In the previous experiment you deliberately and consciously created a state of electromagnetic receptivity in your being. In this experiment you *project* an electromagnetic pattern from yourself to: 1) Other persons, sending them love, healing, protection, etc. 2) Situations, to impart to them vibratory patterns with specific qualities such as harmony. 3) Even to objects, to incorporate spiritual qualities into their material substance. "Blessing" a cross or a home is an example, as is sending strength and well-being to an organ of your own body or that of another person.

For your third experiment become quiet again, regulate

your breath and release tensions as before. Consciously direct the nature of your electromagnetic pattern to flow outward from you to another person, to a situation, or to an object, as you select. To the focal point of your thought mentally project a specific quality—health, strength, protection, love, etc. Try to "feel" the flow.

If you will practice with these experiments for a time, they become habitual expressions. They offer you the opportunity to become adept at creating inner states of being, and outer expressions of being, through conscious direction of electromagnetic patterns, which finally become habitual. East and West do meet. Mysticism and Science are one.

*   *   *   *   *

CHAPTER 8

THE MYSTIC AND THE PSYCHIC

The mystic searches for a relationship with *all* life. He seeks a multi-level relationship with the mineral, vegetable, animal, human and divine levels through his own physical, emotional, mental, psychic and spiritual levels. The psychic level is a "bridge" between the mental and spiritual.

Through the psychic aspect of his being the mystic finds profound insights into all levels of life, both inner and outer. "Now it came to pass . . . as I was among the captives by the river of Chebar, that the heavens were opened, and I saw visions of God," wrote the prophet Ezekiel. This is but one incident of hundreds, described in both Old and New Testaments, in which an individual used his psychic capability to gain an insight into another level of life.

"The light of the body is the eye. If therefore thine eye be single, thy whole body shall be full of light," Jesus is quoted in the Gospel of Matthew. Obviously the statement is symbolic of an inner process. The mystic might refer to the "single eye" as the Third Eye, and agree that if you use it then your entire being will be filled with "light" as the symbol of wisdom or higher knowledge. Your "body," or the physical plane organization of your being, will have the "light," or the spiritual plane organization of your being, incorporated throughout.

There are many who sincerely believe that the Old Testament prophets, the New Testament apostles and disciples, and the divines in every religion were experiencing hallucinations rather than mystical visions. Books have been written to insist that these people were hallucinatory, epileptic, schizophrenic, drug addicts or afflicted with other maladies which were the source of their visions. But with scientific research into states of consciousness, right and left brain functions, electromagnetic fields, ESP, dreams (just to give a few examples) we are learning that previously undreamed of states of consciousness do function within us, and are attainable by us.

As we look at the kinds of experiences which constitute the psychic bridge between an individual's spiritual and mental levels, we'll consider many phases of psychic expression.

¶ INTUITION . . . is probably the most important psychic faculty you possess, and certainly is the most frequently used. Literally, the word intuition means to look upon inwardly. A sudden inner awareness of a fact not arrived at by logic is an intuitive experience. In a previous book, *Adventures in ESP,* (Robert G. Chaney, Astara, Inc., Upland, California; 1976) I've called this kind of inner experience *cognitive intuition*—providing *exact fact.*

There's another kind of intuition which doesn't offer precise information but simply impels you toward a vague thought or an act you wouldn't normally follow. I designate this type as *functional intuition.* It provides *impulse fact* rather than exact fact. For instance, upon impulse you might follow a different route to work in the morning, with some unexpected benefit resulting, or an unknown danger averted, or a lost friendship renewed.

Every person experiences intuition. Some have a greater awareness of it than others. If you've ever known who was calling at the ringing of your phone, you've experienced it on the level of personal relationships.

Dr. George Lamsa translates Psalm 16:7 as ". . . my intuition also guides me during the night." From a mystical point of view, the word *night* means more than simply the opposite of day. It means that fractional moment when the normal consciousness isn't functioning, as though it were asleep, and an impulse from the higher consciousness crosses the psychic bridge into the mind.

Just as the muscles of your body are strengthened by exercise, the expression of intuition is heightened by your awareness of its inner presence and your reliance upon its impulses, whether cognitive or functional.

¶ CLAIRVOYANCE . . . the sense of psychic sight, literally clear seeing, visions that occur on the non-physical level, is another aspect of the psychic bridge which many experience. Clairvoyant visions are not hallucinations. Clairvoyance is a vision of reality. Hallucination is an inner short circuit of the complex human visual system, creating synthetic rather than genuine visions.

There are two principal types of clairvoyance: *objective* and *subjective*. If you were to "see" an otherwise invisible person standing at the entrance to your home, that would be an experience in objective clairvoyance. If the focal point of your clairvoyant sight was centered within yourself, (it usually occurs just inside the forehead) that would be an experience in subjective clairvoyance. Objective clairvoyance is seeing *outside* the perimeter of your physical being; subjective clairvoyance is seeing *inside* the perimeter.

These two types of clairvoyance have their subdivisions which apply in both categories. There is *clairvoyance in space,* in which the beholder sees a distant event. Jesus' vision of Nathaniel under a tree at a distance, and Sweden-borg's vision of the burning city of Stockholm three hundred miles away, are examples of clairvoyance in space. Extended vision is another term designating this mystical experience.

Then there is *clairvoyance in time,* seeing something that has occurred in the past or that will occur in the future, the latter being also known as clairvoyant precognition, or prophecy. Such experiences are commonplace and may be read about in numerous popular journals.

Another subdivision is *X-Ray clairvoyance,* the ability to see within a solid object and determine something of its nature under its outer surface. Would that all physicians might develop this faculty as an aid to their diagnosis of interior human ailments.

You are apt to experience clairvoyance when a strong connection exists between you and another person. Either parents or children most frequently experience clairvoyance about the other—especially mothers in regard to children. Brothers and sisters often have the experience—especially in the case of twins. Where there are strong emotional ties, the psychic expressions are more apt to occur.

Possibly the most frequent type of clairvoyance might be termed *symbolic vision.* One sees a symbol—and its significance must be interpreted or it is meaningless. At this point intuition frequently aids interpretation. Just as the physical senses of hearing, seeing, feeling, smelling and tasting function in harmonious combinations to bring information to the consciousness, so it is true that the psychic senses often function as a team.

¶ CLAIRAUDIENCE . . . clear hearing, is a companion psychic bridge to clairvoyance. It also can be divided into ob-

jective and subjective types. You can "hear" objectively
something outside the perimeter of your physical being that
is audible to no one else. The more frequent type of clairaudience is subjective, often in the form of a voice sound
which in some way is impinged upon the inner auditory
system.

An interesting Biblical comment on clairaudience is found
in the First Book of Samuel. In the first verse of the third
chapter, "And the word of the Lord was precious in those
days; there was no open vision." Apparently clairvoyance
wasn't in vogue at that particular time, and clairaudience
was the preferred psychic bridge.

The chapter goes on to describe how the child Samuel
"heard" a voice which he thought was Eli, the prophet, but
finally interpreted as being the Lord, calling him to spiritual
service, and later establishing him as a prophet.

During the experience, Eli counseled Samuel to answer
the voice and converse with it. If you are having any kind
of psychic experience, *and are assured of its validity,* treat
the situation as you would any normal experience until it
runs its course, or have received whatever you are supposed
to in relation to it.

There are psychic voice experiences (and other experiences, too) that should be ignored. Any time you are obviously misled, or are unduly disturbed, or are so motivated
that you are not in control of yourself, you should inwardly
break off the contact by deliberately directing your full attention elsewhere. To allow interest in any kind of psychic
phenomena to progress to the point of becoming an addic-
tion is to abuse its spiritual purpose and misdirect your own
life. "The spirits of the prophet are subject to the prophet,"
is a Biblical statement which pertains not only to discarnate

entities but also to all the faculties and levels of one's own being. Over-exertion of your muscles in exercise is not wise. Neither is over-extending your psychic faculties.

¶ DIRECT VOICE . . . . a type of psychic phenomenon in which a voice is heard objectively through the normal auditory sense apparatus, not limited to an individual who possesses the psychic sense of clairaudience, but audible to everyone present when the phenomenon occurs.

Biblical instances of direct voice phenomena are found in the 17th chapter of Matthew . . . *and behold a voice out of the cloud, which said, This is my beloved Son, in whom I am well pleased* . . . ; in the 12th chapter of John, *Then came a voice from heaven, saying, I have both glorified, and will glorify it again. The people therefore, that stood by, and heard it, said that it thundered: others said, an angel spake to him;* and in the Ninth chapter of Acts, *And he fell to earth, and heard a voice saying unto him, Saul, Saul, why persecutest thou me? And the men which journeyed with him stood speechless, hearing a voice, but seeing no man.*

¶ GLOSSOLALIA . . . is described in the dictionary as an ecstatic utterance of unintelligible speech sounds.

The Bible distinguishes between "other" tongues and "unknown" tongues. Describing the events at Pentecost it says, ". . . they were all filled with the Holy Ghost, and began to speak with other tongues, as the Spirit gave them utterance." The multitudes were amazed to hear these uneducated persons speaking many languages. ". . . every man heard them speak in his own language." Then follows a list of many of the languages spoken. This is not glossolalia, but speech in a trance state as controlled by the Spirit.

Glossolalia is indicated in the 12th chapter of First Corinthians as one of several "spiritual gifts" bestowed by the Spirit of God for the benefit of humankind. ". . . to another (person is given the gift of) divers kinds of tongues; to another the interpretation of tongues . . . ." This passage describes the true form of glossolalia. Two persons are involved: one who is inwardly prompted to utter speech-like but unintelligible sounds, the other is given the interpretation of those sounds as intelligible ideas.

¶ PSYCHOMETRY . . . literally means soul measuring. In its psychic application it refers to touching an object, usually with the fingers or the entire hand as a vibrational sensing device, then interpreting the vibrations thus received. The object touched may be either animate (human, animal or vegetable) or inanimate (mineral, plastic, wood, etc.). In either event, feelings in response to touching (not the sense of touch itself) act as a psychic bridge between the object touched and the consciousness of the one who touches.

Everyone is psychometric to some degree. Those who become adept at it are often able to decipher the history of an object, and are sometimes able to discern something of the history of its owner, who has imparted some of his own vibratory essence to it. When psychometrically touching a person, the state of physical health and the emotional and mental mood are often discernable.

Everything in the universe, living or not, has its vibrational qualities. Just as an electroencephalograph measures subtle electrical radiations from the brain, your fingers and hands may become a "somagraph," measuring higher vibrational qualities radiated by the object of your touch.

In *The Gospel According to Thomas,* Christ is reported as saying, "Cleave the wood, and there am I." In other words, there is a living, vibratory essence in an object as seemingly inanimate as a piece of wood. Psychometry enables you to perceive it.

¶ TRANCE . . . is a state in which the normal consciousness dosen't function. In a hypnotic trance, the mind of the hypnotist is to some degree substituted for the mind of the subject. In one type of psychic trance the normal consciousness is suspended and a higher level of the same consciousness assumes control of the body and speaks through it. In a second type of psychic trance, the consciousness of a discarnate entity temporarily substitutes as controller of the subject, moving and speaking through the subject's body and vocal cords.

Either of these two types of psychic trance may have produced the Pentecostal phenomena, ". . . as the Spirit gave them utterance." The Spirit may have been either the inherent Spirit of Christ within them or the Divine Spirit that came upon them.

Both the 10th and 11th chapters of the Book of Acts, state that the Apostle Peter "fell into a trance." Clairvoyant and clairaudient experiences followed immediately. Peter saw visions and heard voices during his trance state.

¶ MATERIALIZATION . . . a psychic manifestation in which a discarnate entity lowers the vibratory rate of his spiritual body to the point at which it becomes physically visible.

The 17th chapter of Matthew describes Jesus taking Peter, James and John upon the mountain. Suddenly Moses and Elias, both of whom had been dead for several hundred years, appeared to them and talked with Jesus, who at that moment was "transfigured" with a great, shining light so that ". . . his face did shine as the sun, and his raiment was white as the light."

The 18th chapter of Genesis reveals that as Abraham sat at the door of his tent in the heat of the day, three men suddenly appeared before him. While he entertained them, one of them prophesied that Sarah, Abraham's wife who was many years beyond child bearing age, would give birth to a son. The prophecy was fulfilled.

In the 20th chapter of John, Mary Magdalene looked into the sepulchre and saw two materialized angels who conversed with her. Later she saw a figure which at first seemed to be the gardener, but soon discovered it to be Jesus. This may have been a type of materialization known as *transfiguration* in which the physical features of a deceased person "overshadow" a living person—in this case the features of Jesus over those of the gardener. Jesus spoke to her, so possibly the gardener had been entranced by Jesus for the entire episode.

¶ DREAMS . . . in a purely personal mystical sense, and if not induced by physical causes (such as overeating, hot or cold temperatures, etc.), usually serve one or more of the following purposes: 1) self-reproach, 2) warning, 3) guidance, 4) enlightenment in either an intellectual or spiritual sense.

As the mystic becomes related to ever widening circles of humanity, dreams frequently fall into categories of being 1) symbolic, 2) prophetic, or 3) spiritual visions.

A classic dream that fills nearly all the above designations is described in the 40th chapter of Genesis. The Pharaoh's imprisoned butler and baker had their dreams interpreted by Joseph. The baker dreamed of carrying three loaves of bread, which fell off the basket and were eaten by birds. He was never to serve the Pharaoh again and was beheaded three days later. The butler dreamed of pressing grapes from three vines into a cup and placing it in the Pharaoh's hands. Three days later he was returned to the good graces of the Pharaoh and entered his service again.

¶ ASTRAL PROJECTION . . . a projection of the self away from the physical body, either during sleep or a self-induced trance state. There are numerous laboratory experiments being conducted in this phase of psychic expression. Usually the laboratory scientist confines his experiments to visitations to other points in physical space. The mystic believes it is also possible to visit on higher vibratory ranges of life, the spiritual worlds, the many mansions in the Father's house, inhabited by loved ones and friends, and great spiritual teachers who have entered that domain.

¶ HEALING . . . a psychic activity of many aspects, the healer giving direction and vibrational qualities to the energies involved, the recipient creating receptivity to those energies. It is the subject of the next chapter.

* * * * *

Mysticism is the process of deliberately searching for a multi-level relationship with all life.

* * * * *

SELF-DISCOVERY GUIDE VIII

Meditation is an inner discipline which builds, reinforces and improves the psychic bridge—from your normal consciousness to the superconscious level of your being, or from your consciousness to higher levels of life, or between you and any other form of life.

"Commune with your own heart . . . and be still." (Psalm 4) "Let the words of my mouth, and the meditations of my heart, be acceptable in thy sight, O Lord." (Psalm 19)

There is no one right way for everyone to meditate. From books, courses and personal instruction in meditation, you should create the method which best serves your unique circumstances. *Creative Self-Transformation through Meditation* by Swami Parampanthi is one of the best books you can obtain.

In practicing meditation do not expect, or yearn for, earth shattering revelations or astounding psychic experiences. A superb athlete is not trained in a day. Likewise do the traditional meditation methods allow for gradual but safe and certain evolvement.

There are numerous responses which indicate evolvement of the psychic bridge resulting from meditation. Refer to the following list from time to time, not as goals to seek, but merely as indicators of your progress.

☐ Physical pressure, very slight, similar to the light touch of a hand on your cheek or hair; a band around the head; a tingling sensation on hands, face, or hair.

☐ The sensation of heat or cold to a slight degree.

☐ The presence of light, either white or in color, occasionally in the shape of a sphere, or like a drifting cloud; or flowing streams of color.

☐ The presence of a vibratory force that seems to have no characteristics; in other instances it will seem to be healing or protective in nature.

☐ An overwhelming sense of love totally permeating your entire being on every level, physical, emotional, mental.

☐ A sensation of spiraling upward in consciousness; or a simple feeling of buoyancy, a floating sensation.

☐ A sense of Presence; you have the feeling that someone else is with you even though you are alone. The Presence may include a sense of personality, or simply a nonpersonal presence.

If you encounter any of the above during your meditation periods, remember they should not be experienced to such a degree that they become disturbing to you. If they do, stop meditating or at least decrease the number and duration of your meditations. Remember, too, that not having a phenomenal experience doesn't indicate lack of progress. The purpose of meditation is not to create phenomena, but to increase inner sensitivity and oneness with the Infinite.

* * * * *

CHAPTER 9

THE MYSTIC AND HEALING

Many years ago on a radio program I conducted, I interviewed Dr. Pitirim Sorokin, famed sociologist at Harvard University. He was interested in love—not as an emotion, but as an energy—and the effect love had on body, emotions and mind. He told of startling discoveries.

For instance, he described an experiment which indicates that love is indeed energy. Sensitive recording devices were attached to a yogi and one of his disciples who was isolated in another room. The yogi was asked to project love, and the recording devices indicated he did so successfully. (Incidently he was the first to succeed of many persons tested.) The disciple was then asked to project love, but failed as did so many others before him.

Finally the yogi was asked to project love to his disciple in the distant, isolated room. The reading on the recording instruments attached to the yogi was at the same moment duplicated on the instruments attached to the disciple!

Love is an energy—of measurable intensity and quality. The very idea contains enough potential possibilities to keep mystics and scientists exploring for generations to come.

Dr. Sorokin also discovered that love contributes to long life! He researched the lives of outstanding, religious persons, cannonized by the Catholic Church, who lived in the comparatively difficult time of the 14th Century, when the average life span was much shorter than today. Many of them were martyred at an early age, and of course they had none of the advantages of modern medicine. He compared the length of their lives with two groups in modern society, the hardened criminal serving life in prison and the average person. He discovered that the average life span of the 14th Century "saints" exceeded that of the average person of today and considerably exceeded that of the criminal. The one ingredient present in greater degree in the lives of the saints was love— for humankind, for ideals, for Jesus, for Church.

INHARMONIOUS EMOTIONS AND MENTAL ENERGIES RAVAGE YOUR BODY

Just as the yogi was able to implant the quality of love in the body of his disciple, so do you implant various vibratory qualities in your own body and electromagnetic field. At times what you implant is inharmonious with the vibratory constitution of your body and therefore destructive to it. At other times, harmonies prevail with the resulting increase in vitality, strength and longer life. First let us consider the inharmonies and their causes.

¶ FEAR, ANGER, JEALOUSY, and other emotions which Dr. Sorokin described as "inimical," in other words hostile, unfriendly, adverse, are of a vibratory nature which is in opposition to the normal vibrational nature of your body. That's why today's criminal has a shorter life span than did the Christian mystic in the 14th Century.

¶ INSECURITY is an inharmonious emotional expression that is inimical to your body as an instrument of the spirit. Time after time, persons who've been critically ill have told me that at a certain point they "gave up," not in the sense of losing all hope but of surrendering to a higher will, or power than their own. At that moment a truly mystical saturation of peace and certainty flooded through their being. They could actually feel the response of the body's own type of consciousness, on the physical level, as well as on their emotional and mental levels. From that moment on, physical improvement was steady and sure.

¶ STRESS is another inimical activity. Most everyone believes that stress is an automatic, uncontrollable response to outer circumstances. Actually, with practice, stressful response to outer circumstances can be controlled, calmed, and in some instances completely dissolved. The spiritual disciplines, whether meditation, prayer, devotions, ritual, service to others, etc., and the more modern techniques such as biofeedback and alpha control, are ways to deal with stress—and to minimize or nullify its unfriendly terms with your body, mind and spirit.

¶ REJECTION, too, battles the natural forces at your command. By rejection I mean habitual dissatisfaction with outer circumstances. What the consciousness receives from without is one matter. What it cannot or will not accept is another.

I have a theory about this which may or may not be valid. To illustrate, consider the fact that many surgical organ transplants from one body to another aren't successful. Medical science offers a number of physiological reasons. I suggest that quite possibly a major reason is due to vibratory patterns of rejection created by the patient in his own mind.

He may truly believe that he wants a heart or kidney transplanted to his body. But on an inner level of his mind he is in reality saying, for example, "Someone else's heart is beating in my chest! It doesn't belong there! It can't possibly work!" The mental process sets up adverse electromagnetic patterns too strong for the transplanted heart to overcome. The rest of the body "picks up" on the rejection consciousness and is unreceptive to the newcomer in its midst. Total rejection is the result.

If you will notice those persons who are habitually opposed to others, who are never satisfied with situations or people encountered in their everyday affairs, you will discover that almost without exception they suffer from one physical illness after another.

Inharmonious emotions and mind—let's call it "the rejection consciousness," habitual opposition to people, ideas, situations—ravage and destroy the body. Fortunately there is an antidote for this malady.

HARMONIOUS EMOTIONS AND MENTAL ENERGIES RENEW YOUR BODY

We've discussed inharmonious traits—fear, anger, jealousy, insecurity, stress and rejection—and the ways they rearrange electromagnetic patterns infused throughout your body. We've discovered that inharmonies on one level beget inharmonies on other levels. Let's look at some of the harmonious patterns you can set up within yourself to reinvigorate and reinforce patterns of strength and health on every level of your being.

¶ OPTIMISM. It isn't always easy to cultivate. Frequently you must "work" to create and sustain it. The dividends are rewarding. It meets rebuff by simply changing direction.

It rebounds even from the most staggering blows. Its seed is present within you, inherent with the inner Divine Spirit.

¶ LOVE. Love a person. Love a saviour. Love an idea. Love a pet. Love a cause. Love an organization. Love without reservation. Love with altruism rather than selfishness. Love for what you can do rather than for what can be done for you.

The mystically regenerative powers of love may very well be the most remarkable healing agent in the world. It cannot be dispensed by a physician's prescription. The Great Physician, however, is present in you and gives this restorative elixir to you if you will ask and receive.

¶ CONFIDENCE. The opposite of insecurity. To have confidence in yourself and in the worthiness and worthwhileness of your activities is reinforcing on every level of your life and renders you less susceptible to physical ailments. Confidence, then, is one of the great preventative medicines. Related to and often resulting from confidence is the quality of indifference toward circumstances which seek to destroy confidence. Indifference of this kind is also a preventive against the maladies of life.

¶ RELAXATION. The opposite of stress, which produces tension. Muscles that are constantly taut need the counterbalancing effect which relaxation contributes. The same applies to tautness of emotions and mind.

The finest inducer of relaxation is meditation. The brief moments of actual meditation are carried over into other periods of life and contribute greatly to relaxation. Simple meditation is superior to any tension relieving drug. Meditation allows and indeed fosters the harmonious alignment of all levels of being—all bodies—with one another and with the Infinite.

¶ ACCEPTANCE. The opposite of rejection. Here is one of the great keys to many of the healings described in the Bible, and occurring in churches of every faith and denomination. Acceptance is also a key to healing by medical science. Two persons, treated in the same way for the same illness, respond differently. One is healed, the other is not. Frequently the difference may be ascribed to acceptance of treatment by one person and rejection (either consciously or unconsciously) by the other. The religionist calls it faith.

Dr. Carl Simonton, radiation therapist and researcher on "incurable diseases," investigated the occurence of spontaneous remission—the sudden reversal of an illness toward health without any known medical cause. His research revealed that it occurred in patients whose lifestyles included the harmonious qualities of optimism, love, confidence, relaxation and acceptance. Their attitudes reinforced the atoms of the body and enabled the latter to become victorious over disease. But how does the mystic view the causes behind these differences between harmonious and inharmonious inner activities?

WHAT QUALITY HEALS DISEASE?

Whatever your concept of God, you cannot conceive of God being ill or inwardly inharmonious in any way.

"God is Spirit; I am spirit.

"There is no disease in spirit.

"Therefore disease can be present in matter, or my physical body, only to the extent that I am unable to incorporate spirit in matter. How do I incorporate spirit into matter?

"I must somehow find the essence of spirit and allow it to permeate freely throughout my being."

Probably there are as many formulas for doing this as there are mystics. But the sum and substance of their views can be systematized into the following five steps.

1. *Create the proper conditions* by which spirit comes to the surface of your life and becomes functional. One person may wish to light a candle, another to burn incense. One will wish to visit a church or shrine, another may prefer mountain, desert or seashore. One says prayers, another sings hymns or speaks an affirmation. One likes music, another prefers to center attention on a picture or symbol. There are thousands of ways to create the proper atmosphere.

But remember that *outer* conditions are incidental. It is the *inner* condition that's important. Create the kind of inner atmosphere in which you firmly believe spirit will be present and become functional.

2. *Invite spirit to be present in you.* Frequently and regularly *ask* it to flood your being with its healing, strengthening qualities. The invitation is not for an *external* presence but an *internal* one.

3. *Individualize* spirit in conformity to your personal needs. Your relationship with spirit differs from that of every other person. There is an aspect of spirit that is specially meaningful to you. Exactly what do you want spirit to do in you? Discuss it inwardly in specific terms. You create the boundaries of the individualization of spirit. It is present within you, but it functions in the exact areas you designate.

Spirit is present in you always. You individualize it when you direct it specifically toward a well defined objective. In healing, for example, it may be directed to your heart or some other specific area of your body.

4. *Surrender* is the next step. By surrender I mean that you resign yourself to whatever the working of the inner spirit will accomplish. It means that you are turning over to the individualized essence of spirit whatever it is that needs to be done. You are expecting to act cooperatively with it, of course, but you have given authority to the expert in the field, the spirit within.

Additional directions aren't necessary. Let the spirit function undisturbed. Don't disturb the seed you plant or it never takes root. Surrender with confidence.

5. *Repeat* the first four steps regularly and frequently.

The above is my formula. You should modify and revise it to your own needs. Don't hesitate to make changes. Create your own formula.

VARIETIES OF MYSTICAL HEALING

There are four broad classifications of mystical healing. Most healing occurrences result from a combination of two or more of them.

¶ MAGNETIC HEALING. Mesmer is credited with being the modern reviver of this ancient healing method. He called the energy Odic Force—an energy which exudes from the body of one person, principally the palms of the hands, and is transmitted to the body of another. The ancient Hindu called it Prana. In Christianity it is "the virtue" which passed from Jesus to the woman who touched the hem of his garment.

Magnetic healing is expressed in many forms. The ancients often used a religious relic as a kind of focal storage place of magnetic energy which was later released to the patient. Acupuncture, acupressure, massage, reflexology are all related to magnetic healing.

¶ MENTAL HEALING.   A person who "sends" healing to another by an expression of the mind is engaged in mental healing. A second form of mental healing occurs when a patient mentally directs healing energies to himself on his own behalf.

Mental healing is usually accomplished by simply using the mind to direct a healing "flow." Visualizing a white or colored light around and within an affected area is another technique. Glands, organs, nervous systems and other parts of the body respond to the thoughts expressed in the mind. That fact opens countless techniques and variations for healing with mind. All healing, of whatever type, is in part mental healing. The mind cannot be separated from the healing.

¶ PSYCHIC HEALING.   The psychic healing practitioner places himself and all the energies of his being at the disposal of discarnate entities who in turn direct the energies to the patient. Many ill persons have, with astounding results, called directly upon an individual residing in the next dimension of life for healing aid, usually someone who was a physician in this life, or a religious divine, a great spiritual teacher, or even a member of one's family.

The same healing energies are involved as with magnetic or mental healing. It is simply that many feel that those who reach back to us from a higher life level are more proficient at controlling those energies than we are.

¶ SPIRITUAL HEALING.   In spiritual healing there is an inflow of Divine Power that differs from the magnetic force which is closely related to the physical body. It is involved with spiritual powers of an extremely high vibratory nature, best symbolized by light.

Perception of light isn't limited to your eyes. Every portion of your body perceives light. Research with blindfolded birds reveal that they perceive light through their feathers and into their bodies. Your brain perceives light apart from that received through the eye. More about light later on in this chapter.

EARLY CHRISTIAN HEALING

In Christian mysticism, the first to practice healing were the Essenes. In Aramaic, the word *Essenes* means *healers*. Healing was one of the most important of Essenian activities.

There were two divisions among the Essenes. The *Practici* engaged in mundane pursuits, earning funds to support the group. The *Therapeutici* were principally practitioners of the healing arts.

There was an Essene community at Lake Maoris in Egypt. There are many who believe that the boy Jesus learned about healing at the Lake Maoris community under the guidance of the Essenes.

The Essenes believed that the body is the temple of the living God. They emphasized the concept, "I am in the Father, and the Father is in me," with the strictest spiritual disciplines.

It is interesting to note the direct relationship to the activities of Jesus. He drove the money changers from the temple. He spoke about healing in terms of casting out devils. It seems that in his consciousness, illness could be compared to money changers and devils—the profane, the soiled, the evil influences in the body temple of the individual. If, as many claim, he was indeed an Essene, then it is easy to trace the origin of his healing methods to that mystical group. In the controversy about whether or not Jesus was an Essene, I accept as significant affirmative evidence the fact that his healing methods so closely paralleled theirs.

Most Essenian healing seems to have followed one or more of three methods. First, they were herbalists. They believed that each herb was created for the fulfillment of a need in human life.

Second, they used healing stones and salves. Healing stones (lodestones are an example) either naturally possess a vibrational, therapeutic quality or have it induced in them by persons who are "healers." This is also true of ointments and salves. The Bible tells us that Jesus mixed clay and spittle (forming a salve) which, when applied to the blind man's eyes, restored his sight.

The third Essenian healing method was to induce, activate and focus Divine Power in the body of an ill person. They didn't wait until the need arose, but prepared themselves by strenuous disciplines of prayer, meditation, fasting, bathing, and other methods of daily inner alignment with that Divine Power. By such alignment they became its conveyers and directors.

Another derivative of Essene philosophy is in the matter of secrecy. The Essenes gave much of their knowledge only to initiates in their order. What is the mystical need for secrecy?

THE REASON FOR SECRECY

Jesus evidently accepted secrecy as an important factor in some healings. "And he charged them straitly that no man should know it . . ." states the Gospel of Mark after describing the healing of Jairus' daughter.

"See that no man know it," said Jesus to the two blind men whose eyesight he had just restored. Obviously people in that small community were going to know of the miracle, so why the command to be secretive and not discuss it?

It's a most logical assumption (I can say from personal experience) that his intent could be explained in the following words:

"Don't get into conversation about this with people who will try to take its value away from you. They will say such things as, 'Your eyesight would have returned anyway.' Or, 'You really weren't blind in the first place.' Or. 'Do you think it will really last? I know a person who went blind again.' Or, and this is most frequent, 'This fellow is in league with Satan. Don't have anything to do with him.' "

Jesus knew the effect of mind and emotions on the body, and that discussions such as the above would introduce the lethal element of doubt which could very well destroy the healing that had been accomplished. So he advocated secrecy. "Don't converse with those who will scorn or ridicule or, even if acting from sincere motives, will attempt to cast the stone of doubt at your structure of faith," he could very well have said.

Coping with and overcoming renegade energies, resulting from inharmonious mental and emotional expressions, requires more than one simple healing method. Let's examine instances of healing for the various methods they may reveal.

MYSTICAL WAYS TO TREAT DISEASE AND RESTORE HEALTH

Jesus talked to illness in an individual almost as though it were a living entity. Personification of an illness in this manner is one of the mystical ways to deal with it. You can feel a much closer affinity with anything that is personified than you can with something that remains a non-entity. Thus, through personification, the defiant energies of disease become more pliant and submissive to the conscious will and command of the healer.

The nobleman's son was healed at a distance. Sending thoughts of strength and regeneration through space can be a potent healing method.

The demoniac was healed by "the word." The vibrational force of Jesus' command as he talked to the illness disintegrated its vibrational nucleus and separated it from the unfortunate one in whom it had been residing.

Peter's mother-in-law was healed by Jesus' touch, or the laying on of hands.

The multitude on the mountain was separated from the negativity and confusion of their everyday lives in order to be healed. Separation from negativity gives positive harmonious energies a greater opportunity to function.

The centurian's servant was healed by his own faith. But Jesus activated it and added healing energies to it.

The hemorrhaging woman touched his garment. He then felt a "virtue"—a power, an essence—being drained from his being.

The deaf and dumb man was healed by the application of the healing stone or salve in the form of clay and spittle.

The Book of Acts describes those who were healed by using handkerchiefs as a vehicle for transmitting healing energy from Paul to their presence.

Probably in nearly every instance listed above, we must say that one method alone did not accomplish the healing. Undoubtedly there was a combination of two or more methods.

As part of the atmosphere of healing it seems that Jesus always tried to create a positive viewpoint and harmonious surroundings. "Be not afraid, only believe," he said to Jairus on his way to heal the synagogue leader's daughter. And at his home among the family and servants he ". . . seeth the tumult, and them that wept and wailed greatly." The surroundings were anything but harmonious. "Why make ye this ado, and weep?" he asked. Finally he ". . . put them all out. . . ." When peace and quietness were restored he was then able to heal the girl.

Even the simple act of healing by laying on of hands has its variations, depending upon the kind of thought present in the healer's mind.

As Jesus touched the leper he said, ". . . be thou clean." He modified and individualized the healing energy so that it cleansed the leper of body impurities.

Peter's mother-in-law was in turmoil so ". . . he touched her hand, and the fever left her . . . ." In this case the touch was soothing and harmonizing.

To the blind man he said, "According to your faith be it unto you." This was an act of transferring the quality of faith through a touch of the hand.

He overcame the fear that rendered Peter, James and John helpless with the touch of assurance. "And Jesus came and touched them, and said, Arise, and be not afraid."

Powerful thoughts in the mind are transferred from one person to another through touch. Love, strength, confidence, compassion, harmony, tranquility are but a few of the many positive qualities easily transmitted in this manner. It is all a matter of individualizing the presence of Spirit to a specific purpose.

Hands are focal points for healing energies. They are psychic centers specially oriented to the transmission of psychic energy externally from the body. When persons use them for healing they are apt to notice a magnetic flow of energy from the palms, slight temperature changes (either warming or cooling), the presence of light of various hues. Hands need not even touch another to transmit healing. Placing them upon or within the magnetic field of another person allows the spiritual energy to flow, as does simply facing the palms in the direction of the ill person.

Simple prayer is probably the most universal method of healing. There are two aspects of it which Jesus seemed specially to note: secrecy and receptivity.

". . . when thou prayest, enter into thy closet, and when thou has shut thy door, pray to thy Father which is in secret; and thy Father which seeth in secret shall reward thee openly," was his instruction. By secretly going within your own self to pray, rather than making it an outward activity, you enhance the potency of the individualized Spirit. I've "secretly" prayed for many people who were not aware of what I was doing. It is my personal observation that they achieved more beneficial results than did many for whom I prayed openly.

As for receptivity, he said, ". . . your Father knoweth what things ye have need of, before ye ask him." If that is true, why pray?

The object of prayer is not to tell God what you need. It is to help create a state of oneness and receptivity in yourself.

What happens esoterically when you pray? Probably it cannot be fully explained. But perhaps it can be illustrated in this way: Think of a small, dim light on your left hand, and a large bright light on your right. Imagine that you bring the two together, merging the small, dim light into the large bright one.

The dim light still exists, totally permeated by the bright one. You are the small light. The Infinite Being is the large one. When the union is completed through prayer you continue to function as yourself but in conjunction with the Infinite—and Its powers are flowing through you.

A very effective healing method is fasting. There is probably not an illness known to humankind that someone hasn't healed through fasting. Jesus gave the following instructions:

Moreover when ye fast, be not, as the hypocrites, of a sad countenance: for they disfigure their faces, that they may appear unto men to fast. Verily I say unto you, They have their reward.

But thou, when thou fastest, anoint thine head, and wash thy face; That thou appear not unto men to fast, but unto thy Father which is in secret: and thy Father, which seeth in secret, shall reward thee openly. (Matthew 6:16-18)

But remember that to fast is not only to refrain from food. It is also fasting, of a higher kind, to avoid indulging in the emotional states and thought processes that encourage and create illness in the first place. Fasting from those activities will also aid in overcoming illness.

In Chapter 8 the subject of Astral Projections was discussed briefly as a psychic activity many persons experience. Healing energies are often transmitted to an ill person through this means. When Jesus healed the nobleman's son at a distance, it is conceivable that he literally projected his spiritual self through space to the boy. Many persons "see" those who are sending healing to them, even though they are not present in physical form.

Mental manipulation of magnetic fields is still another healing method. Paul mentally impregnated kerchiefs with a healing energy. The cloths were then placed upon those who needed healing. It is possible to impregnate an inanimate object with a specific vibratory quality, or to modify the magnetic field of an individual directly. Natural forces can more easily function in the healing mode when turbulence in an individual's magnetic field is stilled.

Throughout this book we've explored mysticism as it has sprung from ancient origins. And we've discussed numerous mystical activities as they are now performed. After you check through Self-Discovery Guide IX we'll go on in Chapter 10 to an organized program for the practice of mysticism in today's hyperactive world.

*　*　*　*　*

Mysticism is the art of extending inner receptive capacities beyond the limits of the physical world.

*　*　*　*　*

NEW TESTAMENT HEALING METHODS

Jn 4:46-54............Nobleman's son (faith, word, at a distance)

Mk 1:23-28............Demoniac (word)
Lu 4:33-37

Mt 8:14-15............Simon Peter's mother-in-law (touch)
Mk 1-29-31
Lu 4:38-39

Mt. 8:2-4...............Leper (touch, word)
Mk 1:40-42
Lu 5:12-13

Mt 9:2-8...............Paralytic (word, forgiveness)
Mk 2:3-12
Lu 5:18-26

Jn 5:2-9...............Man at the pool (word)

Mt. 12:9-13............Withered hand (word)
Mk 3:1-5
Lu 6:6-10

Mt 12:15...............Multitudes (separation from negativity)
Mk 3:7-12

Mt 8:5-13.............Centurion's servant (faith, word, at a distance)
Lu 7:2-10

Lu 7:12-16............Widow's son (touch, word)

Mt 12:22-28.........Blind and dumb demonaic (attunement to
Lu 11:14-20   Divine Spirit)

Mt 8:28-34............Gadarene demoniacs (word)
Mk 5:1-13
Lu 8:26-33

Mt 9:20-22............Hemorrhaging woman touch garment, faith)
Mk 5:25-34
Lu 8:43-48

Mt 9:18-26............Jairus' daughter (touch, faith, word)
Mk 5:22-43
Lu 8:41-56

Mt 9:27-31............Two blind men (faith, touch)

Mt 9:32-33............Dumb demoniac (not indicated)
Mt 14:34-36............Many persons of Gennesaret (touch garment)
Mk 6:53-56

Mt 15:22-28............Daughter of Canaanite woman (faith, word)
Mk 7:25-30

Mk 7:32-27............Deaf and dumb man (touch, spittle, word)

Mt 15:29-31............Multitude (on mountain, inspiration)

Mk 8:22-26............Blind man (spittle, touch)

Mt 17:14-21............Epileptic son (word, faith, prayer, fasting)
Mk 9:17-29
Lu 9:37-42

Lu 17:11-19...........Ten lepers (faith)

Jn 9:1-11 ....Blind man (clay and spittle, salve, water)

Jn 11:1-44............Lazarus (confidence, faith)

Lu 13:10-13...........Man with dropsy (not indicated)

Lu 14:1-4..............Man with dropsy (not indicated)

Mt 20:29-34...........Two blind men (touch)

Jn 9-1-11.............Blind man (clay and spittle, salve, water)
Lu 18:35-43

Mt 21:14...............The blind and lame in the temple
                         (Spiritual atmosphere, holy place)
Lu 22:50-51...........Malchus' ear (touch)

Acts 3:2-9 ....Lame man (word, touch)

5:14-16............Multitude (faith, shadow of presence, group consciousness), (Peter)

8:6-7 ....Multitude (belief, joy, group consciousness) (Philip)

9:17-18............Saul (touch, word) (Ananias)

9:33-34............Aeneas (word, Christ presence), (Peter)

9:36-41............Dorcas (prayer, touch) (Peter)

14:8-10 ....Cripple (faith, word) (Paul)

16:16-18............Slave girl (word) (Paul)

19:11-2 ....Many sick (handkerchiefs) (Paul)

20:9-12 ....Eutychus fell from loft (touch) (Paul)

28:8   ....Publius' father (prayer, touch) (Paul)

28:9   ....Others (Paul)

SELF-DISCOVERY GUIDE IX

Your physical body possesses a tremendous amount of natural health and regenerative powers. By giving attention to the factors which you use to maintain as healthy a life as possible, you enhance those powers a hundredfold.

The following checklist is one which I give to persons who attend one of Astara's five-day retreats. I call it the *Eight Basics of Health for the Whole Person.*

Simply read the list to compare with your life activities, then make any changes in those activities you deem necessary.

1. Breath.   Do you breathe deeply enough? Do you regularly engage in breathing exercises?

2. Food.   Do you eat natural, unprocessed food when possible? Do you avoid white sugar, white flour, white salt and chemicals that are inimical to bodily functions?

3. Drink.   Do you drink large amounts of the purest water available? Do you avoid caffein, acid and sugary drinks?

4. Exercise.   Do you do some organized stretching of all your muscles every day? Do you practice any yoga, for example?

5. Slant Board.   Do you spend a few minutes every day with your feet higher than your head? It gives relief from the forces of gravity which otherwise continually draw all your body organs earthward.

6. Meditation/Study.   Do you meditate daily? The spiritual attunement will incorporate higher plane energies throughout your being. Do you study something new each day. When you stop studying, you start dying.

7. Play.   Do you gain occasional relief from vocational and other routine activities by playing, either as participant or spectator? Do you have a hobby?

8. Objective.   Do you always have an objective? Better still, do you always have *two* objectives so that when one is realized the other still stimulates your interest?

*   *   *   *   *

CHAPTER 10

THE PRACTICAL PRACTICE
OF MYSTICISM TODAY

Mystics come in all sizes, shapes and colors. The business-man and the hermit, the housewife and the actress, the salesman and the secretary, all may be "invisible" members of the age old family that partakes of a common, timeless, spiritual strain.

They are bound together not so much by organization or labels but by their common objective: to seek an experiential, intimate union of self with Divinity.

To be a mystic is one thing; to play at mysticism is another. Each individual must decide for himself which he prefers. Whatever "brand" of mysticism becomes your preference, it is important that you be comfortable with it. Any discomfort indicates the unfitness of that particular aspect of mysticism for your specific life.

To be a true mystic, you must in some way, by some method, experience the inflow of Divine Life. The life of the Infinite must not only be present in you, as it is in everyone and everything, but you must become so attuned with it that it has the opportunity to function through you.

Broadly speaking, there are three ways to practice mysticism. The first of them is by *vicarious experience*. The lives of the divines are inspiring, whether they are from the religious or lay segment of society. The example of your

Wayshower passes a portion of its vitality and Oneness into your life. It might be described as passive assimilation of the mystical life.

A second form of mystical practice is *experience through an intermediary*. A blessing, a baptism, an initiation—any of these when conferred and received with true spiritual dedication and sincerity may result in additional mystical experiences and continued expression of the mystical life. This could be described as achieving the mystical life through induction.

The third method of leading the mystical life is through *personal experience*. Your mystical life in this method may include the previous two, but it is also individually your own and conforms to no other blueprint. The Aquarian Age, so we are told, is that time when each person becomes his own priest. This is the mystical life through direct assimilation.

WAYS TO ENCOURAGE MYSTICAL AND PSYCHIC EXPERIENCES

Look at a nearby object, and faraway objects are blurred, out of focus. Change your vision to a faraway object and the nearby object is blurred and out of focus. The photographer compensates for this problem by changing the depth of field of his lens so both nearby and faraway objects are equally in focus.

One way to encourage mystical and psychic experiences is to enlarge the depth of field of your consciousness so it becomes aware of the "faraway" spiritual life as well as the close at hand physical plane life. Other dimensions are brought "into focus," or into more direct conscious realization. They are the different levels upon which you live every moment of your life.

Primarily, conscious awareness is focused upon the physical range. There are temporary "deviations" which center it upon higher ranges. Let there be a better balance between lower and higher ranges comprehended by your consciousness.

A second course to follow is to rearrange your goals, desires and creative self-expressions to accommodate the greater depth of consciousness field you've created. Engaged as you are in materialistic endeavors essential to the continuation of life, it's easy to overlook anything that isn't of this world. You must make inner rearrangements to include other than visible worlds within the scope of your activities.

Millions of mystical experiences are ignored every day in the lives of people around the world. Subtle impressions, leadings, guidings, flashes of intuition, and numerous other mystical, psychic occurrences pass unnoticed through all our lives. So a third way to encourage mystical, psychic incidents in your life is to be alert for significances and correspondences in the experiences you encounter.

Is situation "A" the result of your logical thought, or is its origin on some higher plane? Did thought "B" trickle from your intellect, or did it gush from some higher wellspring of consciousness? Did you meet friend "C" by chance, or did an invisible guiding hand converge your paths?

"Living in conjunct" may be another way of expressing this idea: conjunct with others, with situations, with Cosmic Consciousness, or whatever frame of reference you wish to use. Don't ascribe *everything* that occurs to mystical experience. Be discriminating and analytical. But also be encouraging to your own High Self as it begins to become conjunct with life outside its own. Interactive conversation with higher elements of your consciousness causes them to function that much better on your behalf.

And the fourth practice for the encouragement of inner and higher experiences is to look into and experiment with the mystical disciplines. Adapt and devise your own if you wish, but begin with the traditional. Many of them are described earlier in this book.

BASIC POINTS IN TECHNIQUE

In whatever discipline you discover your own affinity, you will note two basic points of technique.

First you'll discover that the technique is designed to separate your mind from the usual stimuli of the world. In effect, you create a temporary, insulated, isolation booth in which your consciousness is centered. That detached, inner compartment either diminishes or entirely prohibits access to your consciousness by the outer sights and sounds which normally impinge upon it.

The purpose of this technique is to allow your consciousness to become sensitized and receptive to stimuli of a higher vibratory range. It then begins to interact with that range as it previously did with the physical, though with far deeper insights, observations and response.

But before this occurs, you must usually engage in the second technique of temporarily substituting a series of spiritually and vibrationally significant acts. These may include a breathing exercise, adopting a conducive posture, saying a prayer, affirmation or mantrum, dealing mentally with visual symbols and similar acts.

"But none of the above is necessarily spiritual or mystical," many might protest. It's true that they aren't *necessarily* so, but if the mood of your emphasis is spiritual or mystical then these activities become so too. Like begets like is the ancient metaphysical maxim. It holds true on every level of life.

By implanting the spiritual context within your activities, you develop an ever increasing, habitual, intuitive response to Reality. It is life changing, incorporating the spiritual into the material, making the two, one—the true goal of the mystic.

GENERAL FORMS OF MEDITATION

In my objective to simplify and organize mystical matters, I've paid particular attention to meditation. There seem to be conflicting theories about it. But the conflict is considerably resolved by simplification and organization. I've divided meditation into three types, then ascribed a symbol and an objective to each type.

¶ CONTEMPLATIVE MEDITATION is type 1. Its symbol is *the monkey mind.* Its objective is simply *to reflect.*

Many think they aren't meditating when their minds go from one thought to another. Not true. The Hindu teaches of the monkey mind that leaps from thought to thought as the monkey leaps from branch to branch in his tree. All you need do is control the monkey, cause him to pause a few moments on each branch before going to the next. Control your thought. Reflect upon it a moment, then let your mind go naturally to the next one.

Contemplative meditation is a perfectly valid form. It produces excellent results, particularly in the area of harmonizing all levels of your self with one another, and with surrounding circumstances.

¶ *Responsive meditation* is type 2.   Its symbol is the lotus. Its object is *to receive.*

The lotus is the symbol of responsive meditation because it opens itself daily to receive the incoming light. What will you receive in this form of meditation? Perhaps one or more of the following: healing, bliss, ideas, ecstasy, tranquillity, strength, inspiration, psychic contacts, and you can probably quickly add a dozen more to the list.

To engage in responsive meditation you mentally create an inner attitude of receptivity to the specific quality you wish to receive. Try to sense or feel the actual inflow of that quality entering your being and being retained therein.

¶ CAUSAL MEDITATION is type 3.   Its symbol is the candle. Its objective is *to project.*

The candle symbolizes causal meditation because its rays radiate outward from its center. In causal meditation you project something to a situation or another person. What is it? Perhaps healing, harmony, strength, motivation, protection, accomplishment, etc.

In responsive meditation, the energies are inflowing. In causal meditation they are outflowing. One type often merges into another, a process which you should control.

DISCIPLINES LEADING TO MYSTICAL EXPERIENCES

There are other forms of contemplation and meditation that lead to mystical experiences. They will be briefly detailed here for your consideration and expanded use if they appeal to you.

¶ RELAXATION. Even simple muscular relaxation contributes to body composure and fusion of the higher and lower energies leading to mystical experiences. When emotional and mental relaxation are added to muscular relaxation the effect is heightened tenfold.

¶ AWARENESS. Awareness must be centered upon something. It's impossible for the mind to be totally blank. The control of awareness leads to the reception of inspirational ideas.

¶ RECOLLECTION. Recall inspiring moments of the past, not to relive them but to recapture their ecstasy. They stimulate your higher consciousness again as they once did.

¶ IMAGINATION . . . You possess a remarkable imagining faculty with which you can create incidents of tremendous spiritual upliftment. Though they are purely imaginary, they may nevertheless open the gate to actual experiences of a similar nature. Imagine light around and within you. If you imagine it long enough, and intently enough, there comes a moment when reality replaces imagination and the light is really there because you've raised your consciousness to its vibratory level.

¶ VISUALIZATION. An excellent discipline for achieving spiritual upliftment is visualizing a series of meaningful religious symbols—or creating variations of a single symbol. As an example, if you should select the cross as a symbol to visualize, you might go first to the Christian cross, then variations of it, then the Ankh, and so on. Or you could select one cross and visualize it in different settings—in a church, in an outdoor shrine, in a home, a garden, in the hands of a teacher, to give you a few ideas.

Your own visualization is often a step to mystical visualization. Your mental images, if they tend to raise your consciousness to a higher level, may create the inner atmosphere in which clairvoyant experiences suddenly begin to occur.

¶ CONCENTRATION.   This is an excellent exercise in which to engage. The usual example is to concentrate upon an apple, note every characteristic of shape, size, color. Then mentally you begin to enter the apple, becoming aware of the texture and quality of the fruit, progressing inward until you arrive at a seed. Enter the seed, note the layers of matter it contains. Arrive at the kernel. Enter it and come to the very focal point of life force therein and through inner feeling experience its essence.

¶ MENTAL DIRECTION OF ENERGIES.   We are beings of energy. There are energies around and within us. Laboratory experiments show that we are constantly influencing energies whether we realize it or not. Think of the kind of energies with which you are compatible and desire most to use, and influence, in your life.

Energies are basically impersonal and of undefined characteristics. When your mind begins to modify and direct them you render them personal and give them specific qualities, attributes and properties. "The spirits of the prophet are subject to the prophet."

WHAT DO YOU DO ABOUT
MYSTICAL EXPERIENCES?

Those who play at mysticism are ever ready to tell the world each minute detail of their experiences. Uusually the world is bored. Your mystical experience is for yourself and not to be imposed upon any other person.

The enlightened mystic regards his experience as a spiritual treasure—a pearl without price—and in most instances follows the injunction, "See thou tell no man." He shares his experience (to the best of his ability) only when asked, and then only when certain it will contribute to the well-being of everyone involved. In other words, never plant seeds on rocky or thorny soil; plant them where the soil is receptive and conducive to a bountiful harvest.

You should, however, make a personal record of your experiences; a private diary or journal which becomes a travelogue of your footsteps on the path to enlightenment. You will often wish to return to your journal, for the light of future events frequently reveals what was obscure or even totally hidden at the time it occurred.

Analysis of events in your journal often provides additional insights with the passing of time. Even if an entry has no other significance than, "Yes, indeed, this was a mystical experience and I'm delighted it happened to me," your review and analysis of it is worthwhile. It is wise to attempt to relate your experiences to the kind of mystic you are or are becoming.

THE SEVEN KINDS OF MYSTICS

There are seven kinds of people in the world, and they have their counterparts among the mystics. The difference between the normally representative person and the mystic is mainly of degree, motivation, and lifestyle. What are these seven strains of the one human family?

¶ 1. THE DRIVER.   He is goal conscious. He sees the objective and nothing deters him from striving toward it. He is forceful, dynamic, propulsive. He may be somewhat self-centered (not necessarily selfish) in that, to him, all things lead toward the realization of *his* goal.

¶ 2. THE SERVER. The server is humanitarian oriented. He is altruistic, philanthropic, sympathetic, empathetic (which is the psychic faculty of feeling within yourself what others feel in themselves). The server will sacrifice himself on every level to help others.

¶ 3. THE ADAPTER. Here is a practical, realistic person who is alert to existing opportunities for goal realization. He is versatile, especially at combining or changing existing forms and ideas into new ones. He is action oriented, likes to get things done, is flexible and able to adjust to outer situations.

¶ 4. THE HARMONIZER. This person, mystic or otherwise, is a mediator, a peacemaker. He seeks moderation for all, sees both sides of every situation, is agreeable and cooperative.

¶ 5. THE ABSTRACTIONIST. Rearranges the visible, or sees beyond it, to new forms and ideas. To the abstractionist, the visible form world is a starting point for formless and non-visible concepts. His line of reasoning takes him from physical form to an emotional, mental, or spiritual pattern in the consciousness. Principles and laws are meaningful to this person.

¶ 6. THE ENTHUSIAST. The enthusiast becomes excited about his interests. He is the fan, the devotee, the admirer. He may merely observe, or he may attempt to apply the vitality of his hero's or saviour's life to his own. He shouts "Hosanna" at the triumphal entry or cheers at the ball game. Mystical exhilaration is the result of his life method. He focuses on an idea (and it could even be meditation!), a cause, a hero or saviour.

¶ 7. The Ritualist.   The ritualist is a perfectionist, a precisionist, wanting everything in its place. Poets, architects, musicians and many ministers are all ritualists. There must be pure, practical form and meter to all things. He likes beauty, symmetry, accuracy.

At this point we will interrupt this chapter for the final Self-Discovery Guide, designed to help you discover which of the seven kinds of persons you really are, then we'll discuss what to do in the future about your self-discovery.

*   *   *   *   *

SELF-DISCOVERY GUIDE X

You've probably noticed that your attributes qualify you for more than one of the seven types of mystics. You may fit in several or even all the categories. One type may predominate one day and another the next.

Upon analysis—but not a hasty one, please—you will finally discover that one of the types predominates more frequently than any others. That type is *primary* to your life expression. The next most frequently predominating type is *secondary* to your life expression.

To make your analysis, over a period of thirty days, use the accompanying chart in the following manner. Review your activities at the end of each day. Select the category which you feel is nearest to describing your life expression that day. Place a check mark under the proper heading. Be sure to limit your selection to one category only.

Obviously you'll not make the same selection each day, but when you tally up you will have selected one type more frequently than the others. That is the "Way" of your life. That is the primary characteristic of your soul. It is *the way* through which you are expressing the inflow of Divine Life that has come to you.

The second highest in your tally, the secondary category, is *the principal modifier* of your primary way.

All the others are also modifiers, but to a lesser degree. One or the other of them will occasionally predominate, but less frequently. Keep your chart faithfully and truthfully for thirty days to make one of the most important of all discoveries about your self, your life, your mission here on earth.

DAY	DRIVER	SERVER	ADAPTER	HARMONIZER	ABSTRAC-TIONIST	ENTHUSIAST	RITUALIST
1							
2							
3							
4							
5							
6							
7							
8							
9							
19							
11							
11							
12							
13							
14							
15							
16							
17							
18							
19							
20							
21							
22							
23							
24							
25							
26							
27							
28							
29							
30							

Highest total, my primary expression channel is ....
Next highest, my secondary, modifying channel is ....

In addition to Self-discovery, there are three other ways you can use this checklist.

You can study it to fill in what you may consider weak areas in your life, helping you create a better overall balance of the self.

You can predetermine which type you should express on any given day, appropriate to the expected circumstances of that day. You can answer for yourself the questions, "What do I *need* to be tomorrow? What should I emphasize in myself in order to use to best advantage the inflow of Divine Life that comes to me?" Then you can begin conditioning yourself to fulfill that need.

You can use it to help yourself understand others, make allowances for their shortcomings, support their strengths, and increase harmonious relationships.

Thus, you enlarge the depth of focus on your own vision and understanding.

* * * * *

TOMORROW'S MYSTIC

How the picture has changed from yesterday's mystic to today's—from the lone, retiring, isolated visionary to the active expressor of higher energies in all the busiest "vineyards" of the world. What will tomorrow's mystic be? And do?

Heightened ability at telepathy is one of the traits by which tomorrow's mystic will be known. Non-verbal communication over great distances and small will occur with greater frequency and accuracy than today. Even in verbal conversation, by the use of telepathy (and intuition, too) he will possess a much greater understanding of everything anyone says.

All the traditional psychic experiences of the past (see Chapter 8) will be continued, but to a heightened degree. With psychic creativity, variations of all the psychic experiences and phenomena we now know will be instituted. Perhaps the areas of greatest advancement will be in psychic healing, intuition and in astral projection.

A new realization of, and appreciation for, the unity of all life will assume greater prominence, and will result in more harmonious relationships between all the life kingdoms—mineral, animal, vegetable, human, spiritual. Oneness with a stone, a blade of grass, an animal in the woods, another human being, higher levels of one's own self, discarnate beings of high order, the Infinite Being—this is the promise of the future.

The level of conscious awareness was once centered purely on the body, then it moved upward to the emotional nature where it is principally focused today. In the tomorrows ahead, a gradual rise will take it on upward toward the mental and spiritual. This is not to say that body and emotions will be forgotten or neglected. They will simply become better instruments serving the higher nature more harmoniously and productively.

Tomorrow's mystic will possess a tremendous faculty for the mental manipulation of matter. Organs of the body will be under more effective conscious control. Wounds will be mentally treated for almost immediate closure and healing. Nearly instant inner revitalization will be practiced.

A greater interchange of life between physical and nonphysical worlds will be among the mystic arts of the future. Practically at will the mystic will traverse the vibrational chasm between this world and the next, and succeeding higher worlds also. A continuous functional level of consciousness will be maintained during these journeys through the spheres of the eternity domain.

Tomorrow's mystic will more fully engage in the process of "fusing" the spiritual levels of life into the physical. Those spiritual dimensions of life and energy which now lie more or less dormant on the physical level will be activated in himself, and by himself in the beings and affairs of others.

Rufus Jones, the famous Quaker minister and philosopher, said long ago, "The church will become more and more a mystic fellowship." If he was referring to fellowship between lay members, I agree with him, but I feel that a higher fellowship is also needed.

I believe that ministers must be less pedantic and pontifical and more human, less textbook oriented and more spirit oriented, less critical and more supportive, less separative and more unifying. The minister should direct the individual church members from mystical fellowship with each other to the higher mystical fellowship with God. The letter of the law killeth. It is the spirit that giveth life.

Most church buildings are hardly conducive to this goal. The sterility of modern church design needs to be changed so there is a sense of intimacy with the Infinite. You cannot experience oneness with anyone or anything without intimacy. Most churches are designed as tributes to an external God—they should be designed to foster an awareness of the presence of God internal to each communicant.

Whatever its size, let the church, its buildings, its activities, its members, its organization, its ministers be devoted to the truest and highest possible mystic fellowship. When this is done there will come a great Glory in the New Age.

The mysticism of tomorrow will have fulfilled its potential and then, without resting, flow on to the mysticism of the day after.

Until this is done, and after, it is important that you be the temple of the living God. The Infinite Being is in the world only through your being. Your pursuit of the Mystic Way includes a self-assumed responsibility . . . to make that Way harmonious, beneficial, and supportive to all humankind. Your inner journey will have its counterpart in your outer life. The sailing will not always be smooth, but it will be self-productive and rewarding.

—BON VOYAGE!—

* * * * *

Mysticism is the art of experiencing the inflow of Divine Life.

* * * * *